YAS

FRIENDS
OF AC

D0007317

All Shook Up

All Shook Up
THE LIFE AND DEATH OF ELVIS PRESLEY

BARRY DENENBERG

Scholastic Press • New York

Copyright © 2001 by Barry Denenberg
All rights reserved. Published by Scholastic Press,
a division of Scholastic Inc., *Publishers since 1920.*
SCHOLASTIC and SCHOLASTIC PRESS and associated logos
are trademarks and/or registered trademarks of Scholastic Inc.

No part of this publication may be reproduced, or stored in a retrieval
system, or transmitted in any form or by any means, electronic, mechanical,
photocopying, recording, or otherwise, without written permission of the
publisher. For information regarding permission, write to Scholastic Inc.,
Attention: Permissions Department, 555 Broadway, New York, NY 10012.

Library of Congress Cataloging-in-Publication Data

Denenberg, Barry.
All shook up : the life and death of Elvis Presley /
by Barry Denenberg. — 1st ed.
p. cm.
ISBN 0-439-09504-2
1. Presley, Elvis, 1935–1977 — Juvenile literature.
2. Rock musicians — United States — Biography — Juvenile literature.
[1. Presley, Elvis, 1935–1977. 2. Singers. 3. Rock music.]

ML3930.P73 D45 2001
782.42166'092—dc21
[B]   00-068780

10 9 8 7 6 5 4 3 2 1   01 02 03 04 05

Printed in the U.S.A.
First edition, October 2001

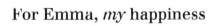

For Emma, *my* happiness

● TABLE OF CONTENTS

● "MARSHA CUP"

Way back in 1957, when I was eleven, my favorite singers were Buddy Holly, Chuck Berry, and Fats Domino. But my favorite song was "Marsha Cup." Every time it came on the radio I turned up the volume.

There was just something about the primitive beat, the haunting echo effect, and Elvis Presley's hiccupy, honeycombed voice delivering those deeply profound lyrics. I, too, wanted a girl whose lips "were like a volcano that's hot."

Later I found out that "Marsha Cup" wasn't the name of the song. It was "All Shook Up," as in "I'mallshookup" not "Amarshacup."

Talk about revelations.

Fast-forward forty years.

I'm doing something I rarely do these days — listening to a live band in a small club near my home in nearly upstate New York. The singer, whom I know, was Mississippi born, just like Elvis Presley. You could hear it in his voice, see it in his style.

Driving home I went to turn on my car's CD player and was instantly transported back to 1957. What happened to Elvis Presley after "All Shook Up"? Who was he, anyway? Underneath the glitter and the glamour, the lies and the legends, there must have been a real person, once.

I spent the last two years looking for him. I read books; studied documentaries; listened to music; watched movies (with *my* eleven-year-old daughter), and saw footage of his appearances.

I went looking for the boy so I could discover the reasons for the strange and sad journey of the man.

Here is what I found.

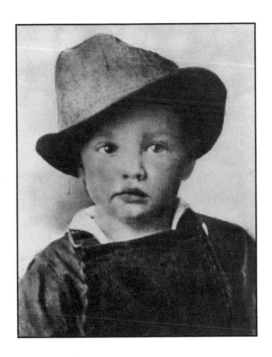

"Before Elvis, there was nothing."
—John Lennon

● INTRODUCTION

Before Elvis Presley, black music was separate from white music — just like black people were separate from white people. It wasn't called black music, not back then. Then, it was called "race music." Race, as in another race. Not the white race. As in you'd better not get caught listening to it.

White music was for your parents. Songs sung by Frank, Bing, Perry, and Tony (Sinatra, Crosby, Como, and Bennett). They were "crooners." Croon: to sing or hum in a low, soothing, evenly modulated voice.

Safe, boring music.

Big hits had titles like: "Peter Cottontail"; "Rag Mop"; "Frosty the Snowman"; "If I Knew You Were Coming I'd've Baked a Cake"; "Oh My Papa"; "Three Coins in a Fountain"; "Come On-a My House"; and "How Much Is That Doggie in the Window?"

There was no such thing as "teenage music." There was no such thing as "teenage."

Blues, the black music of the time, was African music transformed by the horrific American experience of slavery. The blues talked about life and, more likely than not, about its hardness and sadness. It was about as far from crooning as you could get.

Before Elvis Presley there were people (black and white) marking the trail: Johnny Ace, The Drifters, Fats Domino, Bo Diddley, Chuck Berry, Little Richard, Bill Haley, The Penguins, and DJs like Dewey Phillips and Alan Freed.

Rock and roll, the new name for rhythm and blues, was bubbling up, but it wasn't at a full boil. Not yet.

Some white singers "covered" black records, which meant they stole other people's songs. Today it's called "sampling." Black singers and songwriters were powerless to do anything about it.

These white covers "prettified" the music so it wouldn't be too harsh for white ears. And there were lots of white ears. Big-name white singers, backed by big recording companies, could sell lots of records. Money, then as now, drove the music business.

But (and there's always a but) as black music evolved, so did white music. From the country roots of Jimmy Rodgers and the two Hanks — Williams and Snow — rockabilly reared its ugly and unruly head.

Rockabilly combined country with a rocking, driving beat. It was what Chuck Berry was about, strutting your stuff and not listening to the boss man — and the boss man could be your foreman or your father.

Rockabilly was sexy, rebellious, and white.

Then along came Elvis Presley.

A white boy whose complex musical roots were firmly planted in the soil of the blues, gospel, country, and rockabilly. Elvis Presley embraced all four musical traditions and erased the lines that separated white from black — lines that he didn't recognize.

He was destined to take the music one step further.

Like, see, when Elvis came out and a lot of black groups would say, 'Elvis cannot do so and so'... And I'd say, 'Shut up, shut up.' Let me tell you this — when I came out they wasn't playing no black artists on no Top

40 stations . . . it took people like Elvis . . . to open the door for this kind of music, and I thank God for Elvis Presley. I thank God for Elvis Presley. I thank the Lord for sending Elvis to open the door so I could walk down the road, you understand?

— Little Richard

He melded and molded the music and infused it with an intensity fueled by the extraordinary power and range of his voice. He made the music his own — unique and compelling.

And he communicated this feeling to his listeners. White listeners. Lots of them.

In the process he created a national phenomenon. American music and culture would never be the same.

But neither would he.

The fame that engulfed him would, in the end, be too much. For someone so young, it was overwhelming. Somewhere along the way the shy kid from Tupelo with the great voice got buried by the fame he thought he wanted. He became the boy in the bubble and lost sight of himself forever.

PART ONE 1935–1958

TUPELO HONEY

She's as sweet as Tupelo Honey
She's an angel of the first degree

— Van Morrison

Maybe a little *too* sweet. Elvis's mom, that is. So sweet, so smothering and overprotective, he was never able to grow up. That way, she could be sure he would never leave her.

Love, appropriately enough, was her middle name: Gladys Love Smith. She was born poor and raised poor. Her father died when she was nineteen, and she had to help support her four younger siblings (there were seven in all) and invalid mother.

Vernon Elvis Presley, like Gladys, came from a poor family and didn't graduate from high school. Vernon could read and write but consistently misspelled his first name: Virnon.

He and Gladys met at the First Assembly of God Church in East Tupelo, Mississippi. East Tupelo was the wrong side of the tracks and was separated from Tupelo by the city dump. Most of the people who lived there were either poor white sharecroppers or poor white factory workers.

Two months after they met, in June 1933, Vernon and Gladys eloped. Both lied about their ages. Vernon claimed to be twenty-two. Seventeen was too young to get married. Gladys, embarrassed that she was older than Vernon, said she was nineteen, not twenty-one.

They borrowed the three dollars needed for a marriage license.

Vernon didn't have a skill or a trade and seemed satisfied just going from one low-paying job to the next — a "job hopper." He delivered milk and groceries, drove a truck, did farmwork, carpentry, and day labor. Always odd jobs, never anything steady. As his brother Vester put it, he just wasn't "necessarily picky about his work."

Some said Vernon wasn't a good provider. Some said it was the depression — times were hard, and jobs were scarce. No one accused Vernon of being a hard worker, though. He didn't seem to care whether he worked or not and complained about a bad back most of his life.

Vernon was good-looking and good-for-nothing. Women looked at him when he walked down the street. Gladys Smith paid a high price for marrying handsome Vernon Presley.

When Gladys became pregnant, Vernon, with the help of his father and brother and a $180 loan, built a fifteen-by-thirty-foot two-room shack on an unpaved street. There was no electricity. A water pump and an outhouse were in the back. Come winter they stuffed rags in the cracks to keep out the cold.

It was called a "shotgun house." You could fire a shotgun through the front door and the pellets would go clear out the back door without hitting a thing.

At 4:00 A.M. on January 8, 1935, Gladys delivered a stillborn son named Jesse Garon. At 4:35 A.M. Elvis Aron (to rhyme with Jesse Garon) was born. The Presleys were unable to pay the doctor his fifteen-dollar fee. He had to collect it from welfare.

The dead infant was placed in a tiny coffin and buried in an unmarked grave in a nearby cemetery.

The death of Elvis's twin brother weighed heavily on Gladys — a weight she passed on to her son. She took him regularly to visit his brother's grave site. It was a burden he would bear, uneasily, for the rest of his life. Unlike other children, Elvis Presley's birthday would be a day of sadness rather than joy.

Gladys began to put on weight, cared little about how she looked, and became high-strung, nervous, and fearful. Almost everything frightened her. Once, she even had all the trees cut down around the place where they were living because she was sure someone was hiding there.

She talked to Elvis constantly about how he had inherited his twin brother's personality and how Jesse was their own private guardian angel looking down at them from heaven.

Although it could not be known if Elvis's twin was fraternal or identical, Gladys, and therefore Elvis, believed the infant was identical.

As if the experience of losing her firstborn wasn't enough, Gladys soon learned she couldn't have any more children. Elvis would be her one and only. And so he became the main focus of her life. Actually the *only* focus of her life. She worshiped him. She wouldn't let anyone else hold him, not even his father.

She kept him home as much as possible, never letting him out of her sight. Some say when he was a one-year-old, and his mother worked picking cotton, she pulled him along on the sack as she made her way in between the rows of cotton. She was always worried that something was going to happen. He might get hit by a car while playing ball in the road, or drown while swimming. She didn't let him swim, nor did he ever learn.

When she didn't know where he was, she panicked. If she had to go on an errand she took him with her.

They invented pet nicknames for each other and created a secret language. Elvis called his mother "Satnin" and her feet "sooties," like in booties. They talked this private baby talk to each other well past the time he was a baby. Well past.

Making his mother happy became the paramount thing in Elvis's life from a very young age. Their relationship became inappropriately intimate. It was strange.

When Elvis was two his father was charged with forging a check written by Orville Bean, the man who had loaned him the money to build the shack they lived in. Vernon sold Mr. Bean a hog for four dollars and then changed the check to forty dollars ("corrected," in some versions, not changed or forged, since Mr. Bean had cheated Vernon, buying the hog at such a ridiculously low price).

He was sentenced to three years in the Mississippi State Prison and served eight months with time off for good behavior.

Gladys was unable to keep up the payments on the house. She and Elvis were forced to move in with relatives while Vernon was in prison. She had to go on welfare so she could stay home with her son. It was, at best, a shameful period in their lives.

While Vernon was in prison, Gladys and Elvis became even closer. Elvis always slept in the same bed as his parents — not unusual if you were poor in the 1930s — but with Vernon in prison that meant Elvis slept in the same bed as his mother.

Elvis, in his father's absence, was becoming the man of the house.

Even when Vernon wasn't in prison he and Elvis didn't spend much time together. Being poor didn't mean you couldn't play catch with your son or take him fishing. Vernon just never found the time.

My daddy . . . He don't have much to say until he gets
to know you, and then he still don't have much to say.
　　　　　　　　　　　　　　　　　— Elvis Presley

Sometimes Vernon found work far away from home. Most times he seemed more like a boarder than a parent.

Meanwhile, the Presleys got poorer by the day, moving from one run-down house to another. They were so poor,

Gladys had to go barefoot, even in the snow, because there was no money for shoes. Some felt sorry for Gladys, but some thought neither she nor Vernon was worth much.

In a small town like Tupelo, Vernon's prison sentence was common knowledge. Many looked down on the Presleys, and Elvis was well aware of it. He is not known to have ever spoken to anyone of his father's imprisonment. Not ever. In most photographs of Elvis and his parents, he isn't smiling.

● SCHOOL DAYS

Up in the mornin' and out to school
The teacher is teachin' the golden rule
American history and practical math
You studyin' hard hopin' to pass
Workin' your fingers right down to the bone
And the guy behind you won't leave you alone

— Chuck Berry

Elvis Presley heard music even before he was born. During her pregnancy Gladys attended church. She and Vernon had good voices and sang there regularly.

There's a story Elvis's mother told that may or may not have been true.

> *When Elvis was just a little fellow, he would slide off my lap, run down the aisle and scramble up to the platform of the church. He would stand looking up at the choir and try to sing with them. He was too little to know the words, of course, but he could carry the tune.*
> — Gladys Presley

As early as the third grade Elvis sang at school assemblies. In the fifth grade his teacher was so impressed with his singing at morning prayers, she entered him in the Mississippi-Alabama Fair and Dairy Show. The show took place at the fairgrounds, right in the middle of town.

He sang "Old Shep," a real, real sad song about a boy and his dog. He had to stand on a chair in order to reach the microphone.

9

He came in fifth (some say second), which was pretty good, but his happiness was somewhat ruined when his mother whipped him for going on one of the dangerous rides.

His mother walked him to school every day to make sure nothing happened to him and he didn't play hooky. Elvis wasn't exactly dying to go to school. Some say she did this until he graduated from high school; others say it was just until sixth grade. When he was young she held his hand. When he got too big for that she walked on the other side of the street and, from time to time, hid in the bushes.

In the sixth grade he entered Milam Junior High School. Milam was a good school, and its teachers were strict and serious. Elvis got passing grades: no better, no worse.

He wasn't exactly popular at Milam. He was developing and, to some degree, cultivating a reputation as a loner.

3 1833 04076 7441

He was new to the school and was even poorer than the other poor kids. He wore denim overalls while they wore nice pants, shirts, and sweaters. (Once he got rich and famous, Elvis Presley *never*, *ever* wore blue jeans.)

He was shy, awkward, and looked and felt uncomfortable — like he didn't belong. The other kids mostly looked down on him.

In his high school pictures, he's always standing off to the side as if to say he didn't want to be like them even if he could, which he couldn't.

When he was eleven he got a guitar for his birthday. He wanted a bicycle — in some versions of the story it's a rifle or a shotgun — but his mother thought a bicycle would be too dangerous. A guitar would be nice because of his singing. And safer, she thought.

His uncle Vester and the pastor at the church taught him some chords, and by the time he was in the seventh grade he started to take his guitar to class every day unless it was raining. He would sling the caseless guitar over his shoulder or keep it in his locker.

This didn't exactly help him in the not-standing-out-too-much department.

Some of the kids, who weren't big fans, stole his guitar one day and cut the strings. But some of the other kids pooled their money and bought him new ones.

> *He brought that guitar about every day. He liked to play for us in homeroom. And sometimes they let him play at the school assemblies.*
> — Leroy Green, classmate

He sang mostly slow, sad ballads, like "Old Shep," which he sang so often, it became some kind of joke.

Meanwhile, his father went from low-paying job to low-paying job while the family moved from wretched house to wretched house.

Gladys did her best to keep each place neat and clean and prepared Elvis's favorite foods: buttered biscuits, burnt bacon, sausage, sauerkraut and chowder peas, fried chicken, pork chops, and mashed potatoes.

Elvis had already developed some odd habits:

> *Elvis always brought his own silverware whenever he and Aunt Gladys and Uncle Vernon came for dinner at our house — or whenever they were invited to dinner at*

anyone's house for that matter. Elvis, from about age four or five, always carried his own silverware with him, the knife, fork, and spoon wrapped up in a napkin, clenched in one fist. No one seemed to mind, one way or another.

— Billy Smith, cousin

Then one day in the fall of 1948, the Presleys suddenly left Tupelo. The reasons remain unclear. Some say Vernon had to get out of town because of something he did. Others say that he was just hoping to find a better job in a bigger place.

We were broke, man, broke, when we left Tupelo overnight. Dad packed all our belongings in boxes and put them on top and in the trunk of the 1939 Plymouth. We just headed for Memphis. Things had to be better.

— Elvis Presley

Vernon drove the hundred miles north on Highway 78 while Gladys and thirteen-year-old Elvis watched the landscape change from flat and rural to vertical and urban.

Memphis, Tennessee, was a big city (population 300,000). It was where the Presleys would make a new start.

It was where Elvis Presley would find his destiny.

MEMPHIS

Long distance information give me Memphis, Tennessee
Help me find the party trying to get in touch with me
She could not leave her number
But I know who placed the call
'Cause my uncle took the message and he wrote it on the
   wall

— Chuck Berry

The Presleys were flat broke when they arrived in Memphis, and, at first, things got worse, not better.

They moved into a rooming house with sixteen families (sixty people) and lived in two rooms. Elvis slept on a beat-up sofa in the front room, which functioned as a living room and kitchen. They cooked their food on a hot plate. There were holes in the plaster walls, and they shared a bathroom down the hall with three other families. They also shared the place with an untold number of cockroaches.

In September 1949, nearly a year after they arrived, they were lucky enough to be admitted into Lauderdale Courts, a clean, nicely maintained public housing project with grassy walkways and trees.

The four hundred-plus-unit Lauderdale Courts offered affordable housing to factory workers and their families, families like the Presleys who had recently arrived in Memphis and were hoping to make a fresh start.

Their apartment was the nicest the Presleys had ever lived in. They had two bedrooms, a kitchen, a living room, and a bathroom that they didn't have to share with anyone but themselves. (Which soon included Minnie Mae, a.k.a. Dodger,

Vernon's mother. Supposedly Elvis gave her the name when she successfully ducked a fastball he threw at her head during a five-year-old's temper tantrum.)

Vernon, as always, kept to himself. Gladys was more outgoing and made friends more easily, although some thought it was a little odd the way she treated her son like he was a two-year-old.

Elvis's first day at Humes High School didn't really start off too well. As a matter of fact, it didn't really start off at all.

Gladys wasn't feeling well, so his father took him to school, registered him for the eighth grade, and left him outside the principal's office. But Elvis nearly beat him home. He didn't know where the right office was, classes had already started, and since everyone would look at him and laugh if he came to class late, he ran home instead.

The next day, though, Elvis was back in school.

Humes *was* big — a whole lot bigger than Milam. The huge, red brick building was overcrowded with sixteen hundred vocational students. Vocational, as in vocation, meant these students would go straight to work after graduating from high school. No college for them.

Although he joined the Reserve Officer Training Corps (ROTC) and worked in the library, Elvis pretty much lay low the first two years, sitting in the back of the class, and happy to be lost in the crowd. Lost except for his eighth-grade music teacher, who told him he couldn't sing. Elvis politely explained it wasn't that he couldn't sing, but that she didn't appreciate his kind of singing.

The first couple of years at Humes he didn't dare bring his guitar to school. He wasn't particularly popular and didn't go out with any of the girls there. His teachers seemed to like him more than they liked his classmates. As a matter of fact, he was thought of as almost a teacher's pet.

In his junior year he went out for the football team but was thrown off because his hair became a big issue:

> *He came out but he only lasted three or four practices. He had a lot of football ability, but we had rules back then. I told him he's to have his hair cut by a certain time and he just never came back.*
> — Rube Boyce, Jr., Humes High School football coach

His "pretty boy" hairstyle was provocative, and some of the guys threatened to cut it if he didn't. But Elvis just smiled that silly smile and advised them that they could try.

Well, one day they did try. They trapped him in the bathroom, where they knew he could be found fixing his hair. They told him they were going to cut it for him.

Bobby "Red" West, who played center on the football team (and who wasn't afraid of anyone), happened in and put a stop to it. He thought Elvis was a pretty nice guy even if he did look a little different. They became friends for life. Well, almost for life.

It was hard to tell which Elvis paid more attention to: his hair or his clothes. Probably the hair. He was *real* sensitive about his hair, combing it constantly, laying on the hair oil and Vaseline (so much that it turned his mostly blond hair nearly black), making sure his DA (duck's ass) was combed just right in the back and his waterfall pompadour was falling as far forward as it possibly could in the front. He even grew sideburns so he could look like the truck drivers he saw pushing their rigs through Tupelo.

There were rumors that he didn't get it cut at a regular barber shop. Some said they saw him leaving the ladies' beauty parlor down near Poplar.

He lavished almost as much attention on his clothes, shopping at secondhand stores and thrift shops and at Lansky Brothers on Beale Street — a place where few whites went. Sometimes he even bought stuff that was torn but that his mother could make look as good as new.

The fashion coordination was strictly Elvis: black dress pants (nearly every guy in school wore jeans except for him); green, pink, plaid, and polka-dotted shirts with the collar up in the back; and striped jackets. Sometimes, just for a change of pace, he wore a leather jacket with a red bandanna around his neck, truck-driver style.

He either didn't care what anybody thought or was pretending he didn't. Take your pick. He was a rebel without a cause. A true outsider.

He did participate in some things, like the Humes Talent

Show. There were so many students that only the one who got the most applause would be allowed to take an encore, and much to Elvis's surprise, he was it.

It was the first time most of his classmates knew anything about his singing. After that he sang at the class picnic and during homeroom, which didn't exactly make him popular but made him a little less unpopular.

He managed to make some friends at the Courts, though. They played football, rode bikes (Elvis had one by now), and went roller-skating and to dime double features. Sometimes they went over to the fairgrounds and rode the dodgem cars and the roller coaster. Elvis always insisted on sitting in the first or last car.

Sometimes they headed for the bright lights of the big city: downtown Memphis. They were within walking distance of Main Street. Just being there, with all the traffic and crowds, was pretty exciting.

They cruised the stores, nightclubs, movie theaters, went to Pop Tunes on Poplar Avenue, and hung out at Charlie's, the record store on North Main, where there was a jukebox and a soda fountain that made Purple Cows (vanilla ice cream and Nugrape soda).

In the summer Elvis and the boys hung out at the pool, watching the girls go by. When he was alone Elvis liked to read comics: *Batman, Superman,* and his all-time favorite, *Captain Marvel.* He stored his comics neatly in a book rack and only loaned them to kids who he knew would take good care of them.

But more than anything else in the whole world, he liked music. All music: blues, country, pop, white gospel, black gospel, opera, you name it. He talked about it all the time. On Saturday nights he turned on the radio and listened to country music playing from the Grand Ole Opry, telling anyone who would listen that someday he was going to be on it. It wasn't like he was bragging — it was more like he was just stating a fact.

Sometimes he went with his cousin Gene Smith and sat in the balcony of the nearby black church and listened, spellbound, to the gospel being sung at Sunday services. Once a month he went to Ellis Auditorium to hear white gospel music.

At night he would sit outside after supper, fingering the chords on his guitar and singing softly while the neighbors listened. Sometimes at parties he sang, mostly ballads, and only if the lights were kept real low. He wasn't exactly brazen about his singing.

His voice was changing, getting smoother, richer — not quite crystal clear but getting there. He even played with some of the older boys at the Courts who had formed a band of sorts.

He talked about how he hoped to be famous someday. About how, someday, he would be driving a Cadillac.

But besides school, Elvis spent most of his time working.

In his junior year, his father hurt his back (or so he said) working at the paint factory packing paint cans.

Gladys had been working on and off as a sewing machine operator, waitress, and nurse's aide. She worked long and hard to give her son something more than just plain poverty. Elvis appreciated what she was doing for him and wanted to help.

He had been making some money all along mowing lawns, cleaning out gutters, and doing odd jobs. For a while he was an usher, working from five to ten P.M. at the Loews State on South Main, where he dreamed of someday becoming a big movie star. That is, when he wasn't being fed free soda, popcorn, and candy by the candy girl. Unfortunately, this led to an argument with another usher who told the manager, obligating Elvis to punch the usher. The manager fired Elvis. According to some versions of the story, the manager fired all three employees.

Elvis's job working the night shift at a metal company caused his grades to fall, and him to fall asleep during class. The school administrators told his parents their son could not work full-time and go to school full-time. It had to be one or the other.

Gladys insisted Elvis stop working and she resumed her work as a nurse's aide.

Ironically, this caused their income, little though it was, to be over the limit set by the Memphis Housing Authority. They were making too much money to remain in public assistance housing. They were evicted from the Lauderdale Courts and moved out on January 7, 1953, the day before Elvis's eighteenth birthday, taking the first floor of a house not far away.

Four months later, Elvis took a date to the senior prom. Although there was a live orchestra, they didn't dance. Elvis didn't know how. (He never did learn to dance with anyone except himself.) They sipped Cokes, sat by themselves, and left to meet Elvis's friends and go to a party. But the friends never showed.

On June 3, 1953, Elvis Aron Presley graduated from Humes High School. His parents framed his diploma and hung it up. They were proud of the first Presley to ever graduate from high school.

HERE COMES THE SUN

Little darling it's been a long cold lonely winter
Little darling it feels like years since it's been here
Here comes the sun
Here comes the sun
And I say, it's alright, it's alright, it's alright

— The Beatles

Right after graduation Elvis went to work, first at a machinist shop and then on an assembly line. He hated every minute of it. Luckily the employment office where he had registered called and left a message with his neighbors (the Presleys had no phone) that there was a job available at Crown Electric. They were looking for someone who could drive their truck, fix it if anything went wrong, and take electrical supplies to the work sites.

Even though the Crown job paid less, Elvis wanted it because driving a truck was a whole lot more appealing than working in a factory all day.

The people at the employment office told the owners of Crown Electric that, despite Elvis's slightly outrageous hairstyle and choice of clothes, he was a real nice boy. The owners agreed and hired him.

That same summer, eighteen-year-old Elvis went to the Memphis Recording Service, a division of the Sun Record Company (a.k.a. Sun Studios). This tiny, five-room storefront operation was owned by Sam Phillips.

Sam Phillips liked music as much as Elvis Presley — maybe even more. He had worked as an announcer and engineer at a radio station, where he developed his recording and engineering skills. Sam had a very good ear and a very clear idea of what kind of music he wanted to record.

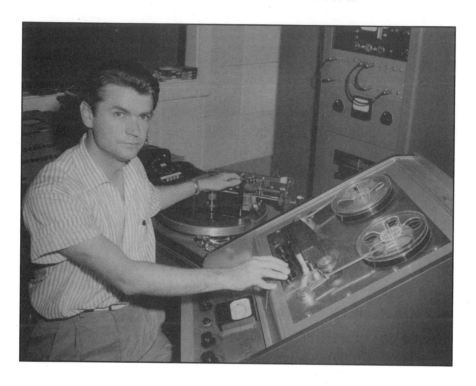

Having grown up listening to black men sing the blues, he wanted to record music that had that same raw, emotional intensity. (In 1949, *Billboard* [then, as now, the recording industry's magazine of record], stopped calling it "race music" and began to call it "rhythm and blues.")

In January 1950, Sam opened his own place and began recording black blues musicians who otherwise would have had to go all the way to Chicago to record (if they had the money).

Not everyone, meaning not everyone *white,* was thrilled with what Sam Phillips was doing. Sun Studios recorded so many black blues singers, it became known locally as "the-chicken-shack-with-the-Cadillacs-in-the-back." Memphis in the 1950s was a segregated southern town with signs for "whites" and "colored."

But Sam never cared what other people thought — something else he and Elvis had in common. He was looking to break down some walls. The walls that said that the blues could only be sung by a black man. He was looking for someone who didn't sound like anyone else: a white boy who could sing the blues. And he wasn't looking to waste time. He knew what the people wanted and he wanted to make hits.

And then, one day, Elvis Presley walked into his studio.

Elvis had come because (a) he wanted to record a song called "My Happiness" as a birthday present for his mother; (b) he wanted to make a record so he could hear what he sounded like; and (c) he wanted to become a singer and be a big star and make lots of money. (The stories, as almost always with Elvis Presley's, vary with the teller.)

Since his mother's birthday had already passed, (a) was unlikely; (b) was almost as unlikely because for twenty-five cents at the five-and-dime on Main Street he could have recorded his own voice and saved himself some money, since the Memphis Recording Service charged $3.98 plus tax to make a two-sided acetate. And besides, the Presleys didn't even have a record player. The reason Elvis walked into Sun Studios that day was probably (c).

Phillips and his assistant, Marion Keisker, were there. In truth, precisely who was there that fateful day when Elvis Presley first walked in to Sun Studios is a point of controversy even today. Some say Sam Phillips wasn't there, just Marion Keisker. Others say it was the two of them. But no one says Ms. Keisker *wasn't* there.

Marion had seen him before, walking up and down outside, like he was trying to get up the nerve to walk in. Marion, who saw to the day-to-day operations (and Sam, if you prefer that version of the story) liked the way Elvis sounded enough to make a tape. Marion wrote down his name and where she could reach him. She asked him what kind of singer he was.

"I sing all kinds," he answered. She asked him who he sounded like. "I don't sound like nobody," he replied.

Over the next weeks and months, Elvis stopped by Sun Studios every once in a while, hoping someone would say something to him. No one did, although they were nice enough.

It wasn't until a year later, in late June 1954, that Marion Keisker called Elvis. Sam Phillips had a song he thought had real possibilities if he could find the right kind of singer. She wondered if Elvis would like to come down and give it a try.

Elvis was down in a flash. Although he wasn't able to do anything with the song, Marion and Sam continued to think there was something distinctive about his voice.

I have one real gift and that gift is to be able to look another person in the eye and be able to tell if he has anything to contribute, and if he does, I have the additional gift to free him from whatever is restraining him.
— Sam Phillips

A month later, Sam called guitarist Scotty Moore and suggested he invite Presley over, play some songs with him, and let him know what he thought.

Scotty and bass player Bill Black had formed a band that played in the Memphis area. They were looking for "something," so they had Elvis come over. Scotty thought the kid could sing, but he and Bill weren't that impressed.

The next night, Monday, July 5, 1954, they went into the

studio to rehearse some more. It was a typically hot Memphis summer day, so the session didn't begin until nightfall. There was no air-conditioning because of the noise.

Elvis sang song after song, mostly ballads. Although he impressed Sam Phillips with how many songs he knew — particularly those by unknown black artists — nothing was happening.

Finally, wired but tired, they took a break. Back from the break, a frustrated Elvis, maybe loosened up by the very fact of facing failure and realizing, instinctively, he had nowhere to go but up, started fooling around. He was singing "That's All Right," a blues song he had heard by a black singer named Arthur "Big Boy" Crudup. Bill Black, no slouch in the fooling-around department, jumped right in, while steady Scotty brought up the rear.

Sam Phillips could hear the change. He immediately

turned on the tape and told them to take it from the top.

"That's All Right" sounded more than all right. It sounded raw, unpolished, exciting, original. Sam took the record to his good friend Dewey Phillips (who was not a relative).

Dewey was the most popular DJ in the Memphis area.

His radio show, *Red, Hot and Blue* (which was) could be heard from ten to midnight on weekdays and ten to one on Saturdays. Dewey Phillips could make or break a record.

Like Sam, Dewey knew that white teenagers, unlike their parents, were listening to black music and would listen to more if they could. And they didn't care what color the singer was.

Dewey was one of the first of the new DJs across the country who were being tuned in to by an increasing number of teenagers with an increasing number of dollars to spend on an increasing number of records played on jukeboxes, affordable radios (twenty-five dollars), and record players (fifty dollars).

In 1956, *Scholastic Magazine*'s Institute of Public Opinion stated that there were thirteen million teenagers with $7 billion to spend. In other words, there was big money going down, and this was just the beginning.

Dewey liked the record, and Sam called Elvis to tell him that he'd better sit by the radio. But Elvis was much too nervous to hang around, so he asked his parents to stay tuned while he went to the movies.

Dewey told his listeners that he thought the record was going to be a hit. Sure enough, as soon as he played "That's All Right," the telephone calls started coming, and Dewey Phillips just kept playing it over and over. (Later, when the way Elvis looked when he sang seemed more important than the way he sounded, people forgot that it was his singing that had first caused a sensation.)

Dewey told Sam to get Elvis down to the studio. Sam told Elvis's parents, who found him in the movie theater.

The radio show was still on when Elvis got there, and Dewey said he was going to interview him on the air, which didn't exactly calm Elvis down. Dewey assured him that as long as he didn't say anything dirty he would be all right.

Dewey asked Elvis which high school he graduated from, because he knew that Humes was an all-white school. Most of his listeners were convinced that the singer of "That's All Right" was black. Now, because of Humes, they would know he was white — just to set the record straight.

Elvis asked when the interview was going to start, and Dewey said it had started — in fact, it was already over. He'd had the mike open the whole time.

● ● ●

Music wasn't the only thing Elvis Presley was working on that summer. Dixie Locke was fifteen, small, with shoulder-length dark hair, an outgoing manner, and a real good sense of humor. They had first seen each other at church and "accidentally" bumped into each other at the Rainbow Rollerdome. You know how it is. Before long they were going out nearly every night and talking on the phone when they weren't seeing each other.

Dixie liked Elvis because he was different. He not only *looked* different, he *was* different. She found most other boys boring.

Her parents thought he looked different, too. Too different. Why did his hair have to be so greasy, and why did he have to wear it so long? And why did his clothes have to look so, well, so outrageous? But after a while they grew to like the radical-looking boy who seemed sincere, honest, and well-meaning, appearances to the contrary.

Sometimes they would double-date with Elvis's cousin Gene and go to K's Drive-In, calling their orders out the window into the two-way radios and waiting for the carhops to bring their deluxe cheeseburgers, french fries, and thick milk shakes.

They went to all-night gospel sings or the movies, baby-sat, watched TV together, or just sat on her front porch while he sang to her.

He took her to the junior prom and gave her his class ring. Sometimes they talked about serious things — like his twin brother. And they talked about getting married someday.

Then his record started to catch on, he began to tour, and things started to fall apart.

When he was away she would spend time with his mother. Dixie grew to like Mrs. Presley but thought that Elvis would never, ever leave home as long as she was alive.

When he called, Elvis and Dixie argued. Elvis was *very* possessive and *very* suspicious. If she wasn't home when he called from the road, he wanted to know where she had been. Who she had been with. Usually she was just out with her girlfriends listening and dancing to records on the jukebox. She didn't want to just wait around for him to come home. Sometimes he was gone for two weeks at a time. And, besides, the real question was what was *he* doing while he was out there playing in front of all those screaming girls. One time she even gave him back his class ring.

Dixie saw that things were changing. Touring and his new career were tearing them apart. He was heading someplace she didn't understand. Didn't want to understand. She wished it wasn't so, but knew it was.

And there was no way to stop it.

● SENSATION

You'll feel me comin'
A new vibration
From afar you'll see me
I'm a sensation

— The Who

Within days of the Dewey Phillips show, Sun had received thousands of orders for Elvis's record. "Blue Moon of Kentucky" — as good as "That's All Right" in its own way — was the B side. Elvis, Scotty, and Bill began playing the Memphis music scene — places like the Bon Air Club and the Eagle's Nest ("Don't Wear a Tie Unless Your Wife Makes You" was

their motto). For the opening of the new Airways shopping center they played on a flatbed truck in the parking lot in front of Katz's Drugstore, drawing a surprisingly large crowd.

Sam Phillips managed, despite Elvis's age (nineteen) and lack of experience, to get him a spot on Nashville's Grand Ole Opry. Elvis's appearance, however, turned out to be less than grand. The conservative, older country crowd just didn't get it. Some folks thought it was a bit odd that he was wearing black mascara and blue eye shadow. The manager told him he shouldn't quit his day job (which didn't exactly boost Elvis's fragile ego — he remembered the comment, unfondly, for decades).

At the Grand Ole Opry, Elvis was in country music's mecca. And at that time, country music was so conservative, drummers could be heard but not seen — if you had one, he had to play behind the curtain. Electrified instruments had been forbidden for years. Elvis's style just didn't fit their mold, musically or otherwise. It didn't fit anyone's mold.

But two weeks later, appearing at the Opry's more adventurous competition, the Louisiana Hayride, otherwise known as "The Cradle of the Stars," he was a genuine success. The Hayride was broadcast live over the radio every Saturday night, and Elvis began appearing regularly, signing a one-year contract.

"That's All Right"/"Blue Moon of Kentucky" was on its way to becoming a hit single, even getting airplay outside of Memphis in New Orleans, Dallas, Houston, and Little Rock. But it hadn't been easy.

Rhythm and Blues stations thought he sounded too country, and, besides, wasn't this guy white? And country stations wouldn't play it because it sounded too r&b/black. They didn't play that kind of stuff, and besides, "Elvis" was a black name, wasn't it?

For the next two and a half years, Elvis, Scotty, and Bill traveled nearly nonstop, racking up 100,000 miles and playing hundreds of dates (many with his name misspelled: Ellis, Alvis, Pressley, Prestley).

Each week they would head for Shreveport to do the Hayride (fifty appearances over the next two years), then Elvis would go home for a day or two, record for Sun, see Dixie and his folks, and be back out on the road before he knew it.

They would strap Bill's bass to the roof of the car (the three of them had quit their jobs by now) and drive the two-lane blacktops and rural dirt roads that crisscrossed Texas and the South. They played in junior colleges, high school gyms, armories, nightclubs, and roadhouses — and those were the big venues.

He was "crossing over," appealing to pop, country, and r&b fans. It didn't matter. Like he told Marion Keisker, he didn't sound like nobody, and he didn't.

Elvis Presley was going where no one had gone before, not knowing or caring about the obstacles he would meet on the way and armed only with an instinctive, inarticulate musical vision.

Of course, before the realization of every good vision (musical or otherwise) comes lots of hard work. Sam Phillips wanted Elvis to hit the road. Supporting airplay with live performances was the only way to sell records, and that was what this was all about.

They would drive to a town, do the show (or shows — sometimes they played two a day, "doubleheaders," and even one known "triple-header"), jump in the car, drive all night, arrive in the next town — when they arrived depended on speeding tickets and car trouble — collapse, sleep (maybe) for a couple of hours, have breakfast (when everyone else was having dinner), play the next gig, pack up, and head out.

Sometimes they arrived in the next town with only enough time left to go on.

Elvis would come out dressed to kill: black pants with a pink stripe down each leg, and a matching pink jacket; green silk shirts; multicolored cowboy shirts; tuxedo jackets; and red pants.

He would just stand there with that big grin (or was it a sneer?) on his face, his blue eyes sparkling mischievously (whatever it was, it was *attitude* about fifty years early). Maybe he would spit out his gum. Maybe just hold the mike, looking out at the crowd, and you'd never believe that just seconds before he had been nearly paralyzed with stage fright.

Then he would just rise up on his toes and explode (there was no other way to describe it) — not even bothering to give Scotty or Bill a nod. He would just go right *into* the music, hitting his guitar so hard, he would break a string, moving his hips and legs crudely or sensually, depending on your point of view.

He was perfecting his stage performance, becoming more confident with each show, making sure he maintained contact with his audience. Contact, hell, they were standing on their chairs, half frantic, over every little thing he did. He made mental notes of it all. Shaking his left leg seemed to generate an awful lot of excitement, and everyone, especially the fifteen-year-old girls (and that was just about everyone), would start screaming every time he did it. It seemed like once

they started they would never stop. Couldn't stop even if they wanted to, so he just kept doing it.

"Hysteria," it was called. It got so crazy, the band couldn't hear what they were playing half the time.

Sometimes it was so out of control, it was truly frightening. Like the time in Jacksonville, Florida, when he made the mistake of telling all the girls he would meet them backstage, and about half of them took him up on it right then and there and stampeded down from the stands, overwhelmed the police, cornered him in his dressing room, and ripped his clothes to shreds.

A year later, returning to Jacksonville, Elvis was warned by authorities that he would be arrested if his performance was as lewd and vulgar as last year's.

Elvis turned the whole thing into a joke: not moving his body an inch, and wiggling his pinkie finger in sync with the recently added drums as the crowd roared with approval.

He even dedicated the last number to the judge who — along with a committee of concerned citizens, can't you just see their faces? — was watching the first show before allowing Elvis to do the next one, which he did.

He liked to flirt, and now, with an audience full of girls, well, it was like he had died and gone to heaven. No, this was better than heaven. Heaven couldn't be this good. Sometimes, though, the girls' boyfriends didn't appreciate what was going on, and that became a whole different problem.

Headliners wouldn't go on after him. Soon, bands refused to appear on the same bill because they knew that Elvis was the one everyone was waiting for.

His live shows were generating more heat than his records. The shows were so wild sometimes, it took him all night to unwind.

Elvis always had lots of nervous energy, even before he started to perform in front of an audience: pacing, biting his nails, drumming his fingers, shaking his legs.

Now his body felt electrified, plugged-in, like Scotty's guitar. He was usually nervous before a show and pretty much stayed that way for hours afterward, thanks in part to No-Doz and his mother's diet pills.

He was always keyed up. . . . We would want to go to sleep. Elvis was so full of energy he wanted to stay up and talk all night.

— Scotty Moore

It was impossible to sleep. He was too wired. Sometimes he wouldn't fall asleep until dawn. He always had problems sleeping, even when he was little. It began when his father was sent to prison. He started sleep walking, once making it all the way to the top floor of the apartment building. His mother had to have the inside knob removed from his bedroom door.

Every night he called his mother from the road. She was proud of him and began keeping a scrapbook. She was proud, but she was worried. Worried by all this talk about the way Elvis moved when he sang. Anybody in the family could tell you he got his rhythm from her, so what could be bad about that? When she was a teenager herself she was quite a good buck dancer, and buck dancing was done alone, just like her boy was doing up there on the stage.

But that wasn't all she was worried about. She was worried even more about this new lifestyle her boy was leading. Worried where it was heading and that maybe it was heading there a little too fast. It sure seemed like that to her. (Forget Vernon — he just told Elvis to learn to be an electrician and give up this guitar stuff, because playing the guitar never got anyone anywhere, at least according to Vernon.)

It sure was nice when Elvis got that first royalty check from Sun, though. *Two hundred dollars*. And the first thing he did was go right out and buy his mother a nice dress and shoes.

The money started to burn a hole in his pocket (it always would), so he headed for Lansky Brothers on Beale. Beale Street was Main Street if you were black, and Lansky's was where most of the black musicians bought their flashy clothes, and that was good enough for Elvis. Lansky's was the best. He used to do more looking than buying (so much that the owners

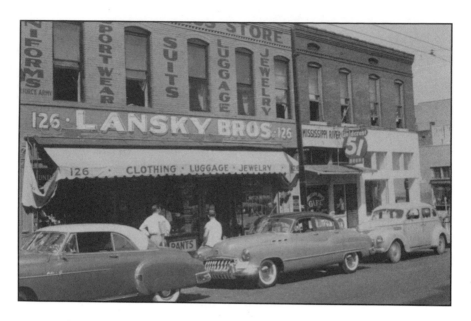

recognized him even before he became famous), but not now. Now it was strictly cash-and-carry, and price was no problem.

The Presleys had money now for the first time in their lives. A four-room house with the furniture to go with it and a brand-new car for his mother. And not just any car, but the pink Cadillac she had dreamed about her whole life. It was too bad she couldn't drive (never did and never would), but that wasn't the point, was it?

She was happy about the money, but she was concerned, too. Frightened, even. She had held on to him for so long, and now she didn't even know which state he was in half the time (geographically speaking).

She was losing her baby, she could see that.

Articles began appearing. *Billboard* called Elvis "a potent new character who can sock over a tune for either the country or the r&b markets . . . a strong new talent."

There were stories about how he was Sun's new star (this was before everyone was a star and every star a superstar) and about his meteoric rise. (Since most of the article writers hadn't traveled with him the past two years, they didn't know much about all the hard work that was behind constant touring.)

Maybe it was a meteoric rise, Elvis thought, but frankly it was moving so fast, he wasn't even getting a chance to enjoy it or even see what was happening.

But there were other articles. Articles written by people who were offended and outraged. They described his performances as striptease shows with clothes on. He'd better clean up his act, they warned, and there was an "or else" in there somewhere.

This wasn't just some kind of weird music they didn't understand (although God knows they didn't understand). No, this was something entirely different. Something threatening. Dangerous.

Elvis Presley concerts were banned in Jersey City, New Jersey (bad for the community); a convention of high school principals meeting in the nation's capital voted to ban his records at all future sock hops; Cleveland officials found an ancient ordinance forbidding anyone under eighteen from dancing in a public place; in San Antonio rock and roll wasn't allowed near the city's swimming pools. A Long Island teenager, grabbing her baby-sitting money and not much else, ran away from home because her parents wouldn't let her play Elvis Presley records (she made it all the way to Memphis); DJs smashed his records on the air; and in Cincinnati a car dealer promised to do the same in your presence if you bought a new car: Come on down.

Preachers denounced him from their pulpits on Sundays

(immoral corrupter of youth), and eight girls were suspended from their Catholic school just for attending one of his shows.

And studies showed. Studies showed that just listening to Elvis Presley records could make you deaf. Can you imagine?

According to psychiatric experts, Elvis fans were "misfits" at best, and possibly "hardened criminals."

There were even stories surfacing about how some of the girls were asking him to autograph their bras, breasts, and panties. Even more incredibly, they were carving his name into their arms with knives.

People wrote letters to the FBI saying they were certain he was endangering the security of the country, and there were threats on his life.

Across the country, the media attacked Elvis Presley with a vehemence that had not been seen before or since.

Elvis tried to explain that he wasn't trying to do anything "lewd," as they called it. Or even sexy. It was just how he sang, how he expressed himself. Moving his body was part of the singing, not something he did separately.

Perhaps, and he didn't exactly say it like this, perhaps they were reading a little too much into it. It was just music.

But no one was listening to him; they were too concerned. This new kind of music was causing race mixing, rioting, juvenile delinquency, disrespect, and rebellion — didn't all the kids start talking back around the time of his first record?

Hell, this was destroying *society as we know it,* and no one wanted that, certainly no one over eighteen.

This was bad.

This was rock and roll.

COME TOGETHER

Here come old flattop, he come groovin' up slowly
He got ju ju eyeball
He one holy roller
He got hair down to his knees
Got to be a joker, he just do what he please
Come together
Right now
Over me

— The Beatles

It was happening fast, but Elvis was still only a regional, not a national, phenomenon. If he wanted to break out of the South, he would need some serious management.

Scotty Moore had been their manager, but besides not having the necessary experience, he wanted to concentrate on playing his guitar, not booking club dates. Bob Neal, a Memphis DJ and promoter, became manager after Scotty. Neal was married and the father of five boys, so he didn't want to be on the road and away from his family.

Sam Phillips had Sun Studios to run and didn't want to manage anyone. And Elvis — well, the only thing he knew about the business was that he hated it.

If Elvis was to become a national singing sensation, they needed someone and they needed him now.

Enter the Colonel: Thomas A. Parker.

The Colonel wasn't really a colonel — it was an honorary commission given to him by the state governor. But honorary or not, he insisted everyone call him that.

Not only wasn't he a real colonel, he wasn't even a real

American, although no one knew that in 1954. His real name was Andreas Cornelis Van Kuij. He was born in Holland and had entered the United States illegally.

He wasn't exactly your average-looking guy.

He wore baggy suits that looked as wrinkled and rumpled as he did; was beady-eyed, big (at one point weighing three hundred pounds), had a jowly, overly large oval face that more often than not had a cigar stuck in it.

But his looks were deceiving. He was nobody's fool. Quite the contrary. He was outgoing, hardworking, shrewd, slick, aggressive, and fearless.

He had joined a carnival in his twenties and become semi-famous for:

- Selling foot-long hot dogs with bits of meat sticking out of either end of the bun but nothing in the middle.
- Painting sparrows yellow and selling them to the suckers who thought they were buying canaries.
- Spreading cow manure on the paths leading from the exits so that the fools leaving the tent shows would feel compelled to rent one of his ponies in order to ensure a more pleasant journey.
- And, of course, there were his dancing chickens that strutted to the tune of "Turkey in the Straw" to avoid burning their feet on the hot plate Parker had hidden under the straw.

After the carnival stint he became Tampa, Florida's head dogcatcher, running a pet cemetery on the side. He offered the bereaved pet owners perpetual fresh flowers on the grave site. However, he neglected to inform them that he got the flowers free from a local florist because they were so wilted. If someone came by to visit their pet's resting place, Parker would just tell them it was too bad they hadn't come a day or two earlier when the flowers were so fresh, it would make your heart go pitter-patter.

From dogcatcher, it was a natural progression to show business, and Parker ran a Nashville-based booking and talent agency specializing in country singing stars.

Bob Neal was using Parker and his booking agency to line up shows for Elvis. The Colonel had been checking Elvis out. The word was that this kid might be someone Parker was interested in, and he was. More impressive than Elvis's performance (not that he wasn't impressed) was the reaction of his audiences. Even the Colonel had never seen anything quite like that before.

Parker perceived Elvis as hardworking and ambitious, like him. Most important, he figured him as someone who would do as he was told. The Colonel liked people who would do what they were told.

He started to slip Elvis extra money after a show — two hundred, say — telling him that this was the kind of money he could be making if he signed with him.

He told Elvis about all the *big* plans he had for him: bigger venues, bigger contracts with big record companies, TV appearances, and something that Elvis had fantasized about maybe even more than being a famous singer: becoming a movie star.

Elvis wanted to be famous and he saw Parker as the man who could bring him that fame.

Vernon had already been won over (which was important because twenty-year-old Elvis was still a minor, and his parents would have to sign the contract). Vernon's pupils turned into dollar signs every time he heard Parker's plans. He was interested in making as much money as possible, as fast as possible, any way possible.

There was only one problem, and her name was Gladys.

Gladys hated Parker from day one. "I don't trust him. He's a cigar-smoking shyster." She didn't understand why her son had to get mixed up with someone like him when he could remain with nice, trustworthy people like Bob Neal and Sam Phillips.

In order to win Gladys over, Parker had Hank Snow, his number one client and the biggest country singer at the time, come over to the Presley house for a visit. It was a *very big deal,* and Snow did a good snow job on Gladys. Good enough that the Colonel could now turn his attention back to *the deal.*

The deal was delicate, complicated, convoluted, and costly. Just the kind of deal the Colonel liked best. *The deal* not only involved taking over as Elvis's manager but getting him away from Sun Records.

It's hard to say who hated Parker more, Sam Phillips or Gladys. Phillips, being a little wiser in the wicked ways of the world, probably had the edge here. (He never did call him "Colonel.")

Phillips believed that Elvis would be making a mistake if he signed with someone like Parker.

But there were things involved here that didn't have to do with managing Elvis Presley. Sam Phillips was seriously considering selling Elvis's recording contract, if the price was right.

At the time no one, not even Sam, could foresee the enormity and longevity of what would become Elvis Presley's career. It hadn't happened before, and it hasn't happened since.

. Ironically, Elvis's extraordinary success was placing small Sun Studios in a precarious financial position. They were overextended. If Sam Phillips stayed with Elvis, he would be gambling everything on just one person — something he wasn't sure he wanted to do. He had other young recording artists he wanted to work with. Artists he thought were just as talented as Elvis.

If Sam Phillips was going to sell Elvis's contract, he wanted top dollar. Although there were offers, the execs at the major labels said his asking price was too high. No one's contract could be worth $20,000, they said, and walked away. (To some degree Phillips's high asking price reflected his own misgivings about selling Elvis's contract. Maybe if he insisted on enough money no one would take him up on it.)

But now, with Parker and his connection to RCA, a major label, the price was starting to look right. Real right.

Eventually, by late 1955, they had worked out the details. Phillips sold Presley's contract to RCA in a deal brokered by Presley's new manager, Colonel Tom Parker.

RCA paid $35,000 to Sun, the highest price ever paid for a recording contract.

The Presleys did not consult a lawyer before signing.

Elvis Presley went with Colonel Tom Parker despite the strong negative feelings of the two people he (rightly) trusted most in the world: his mother and Sam Phillips.

The decision is a disturbing one for that reason. The only explanation is that years of poverty coupled with the promise of fame and fortune being dangled before the twenty-year-old's eyes made it simply too hard too resist.

In November 1955, Elvis sent a telegram to Parker. It is eerie and prophetic:

DEAR COLONEL,
WORDS CAN NEVER TELL YOU HOW MY FOLKS AND I APPRECIATE WHAT YOU DID FOR ME. I'VE ALWAYS KNOWN AND NOW MY FOLKS ARE ASSURED THAT YOU ARE THE BEST, MOST WONDERFUL PERSON I COULD EVER HOPE TO WORK WITH. BELIEVE ME WHEN I SAY I WILL STICK WITH YOU THROUGH THICK AND THIN AND DO EVERYTHING I CAN TO UPHOLD YOUR FAITH IN ME.

AGAIN, I SAY THANKS AND I LOVE YOU LIKE A FATHER.
ELVIS PRESLEY

Sadly, he would keep his promise.

From this point on, the Colonel became the dominant influence in Elvis's life. An influence that was seen as a good one for twenty years but which was, in fact, ill-fated and destructive.

But no one (except maybe Gladys and Sam) knew that then. And no one knew that, musically, Elvis Presley's best years were over.

My music wasn't the same after Sun.

— Elvis Presley

● MONEY

The best things in life are free
But you can keep them for the birds and bees
Now give me money
That's what I want

— The Beatles

The Colonel wasn't wasting any time.

He had already developed a master plan: Elvis was a commodity to be packaged, marketed, and sold in a way that made the most money in the shortest period of time with the least effort. Subtleties like artistic taste and vision, personal growth and integrity, inner gratification, and even long-term goals were not part of Parker's plan.

With the Colonel's controlling but canny management driving him, Elvis Presley would become the first performer to fully exploit the new electronic media: radios (by 1956 there were approximately 100 million in the United States), record players (with cheap 45s taking over 78s, record sales would more than double between 1954 and 1958), movies, and the latest of the new media, television.

Television was the "Yellow Brick Road" that led to *national exposure,* and that, as everyone knew (certainly someone like former carnival barker Parker), was just a stone's throw from *the land of big bucks,* which was precisely where they were heading.

First there were six appearances on CBS's *Stage Show* (at $1,250 a pop). Next came two appearances on *The Milton Berle Show* ($5,000 per). The second appearance, before 40 million viewers, resulted in outraged cries that he was vulgar, tasteless, appalling, and had single-handedly caused American

music to sink to a new low. Most cruel, according to *The New York Times* he clearly didn't know how to sing.

By the time he appeared on *The Steve Allen Show,* the controversy over his evil influence on America's female teenage population had, like them, reached a fever pitch.

Comedian and smart-aleck Allen, smug as always, attempted to have his cake (Elvis and the ratings) and eat it, too (i.e., not take too much heat).

Elvis, in the first of what would become a lifelong pattern of sadly acquiescent decisions, agreed to do a sketch that made fun of hillbillies — or southerners in general, depending on how you looked at it. But either way it was odd. Elvis was both a hillbilly and a southerner. Why did he do it?

Maybe money? Forty dollars a week driving a truck for Crown, or $7,500 for acting the fool on national TV for a few minutes. You do the math.

And that wasn't all.

To sing "Hound Dog," his latest single, Elvis stood perfectly still (as he was directed) in a formal tuxedo (to show how refined and civilized he was). Then, as if that wasn't enough, he sang to a top-hatted basset hound who looked about as bored as he did, possibly due to the white bow ties they both were wearing.

The next day, fans picketed the studio with signs saying that they wanted the real Elvis, unaware that the real Elvis was slipping away a little each day.

Now Elvis was ready for the "really, really big show": Ed Sullivan, the reigning king of Sunday-night-family-viewing-network TV. *The* top rated hourly show featuring a parade of jugglers, dancers, singers, actors, comedians, and whoever was hot that week.

Sullivan, who was even more of a "square" than Allen, hated Elvis and swore he would never have him on the show. But, after seeing his competitor Allen's ratings (the Presley appearance was the first time Allen had beaten Sullivan in the ratings), he booked him for three shows at an astounding and then-unheard-of $50,000.

You could almost see the Colonel licking his ample chops.

The first show pulled an incredible 82.6 percent: 54 million people. One-third of the nation and the biggest TV audience ever. (There were also 25,000 requests for tickets to the theater.)

On his third and final appearance, the cameras shot Elvis from the waist up to avoid the instant decline of *society as we know it,* not to mention the unsettling spectacle of teenage girls running wild in the streets.

Sullivan, who had stood on the sidelines watching and muttering to himself, had seen the light (light here is defined as Ratings x Advertising = Money) and told America that Elvis was a real fine boy, so they would quit worrying about what was going to happen now that this cretin was doing his thing not just in southern towns no one ever heard of but, thanks to the miracle of TV, in your living room.

I remember when I was nine years old and I was sittin' in front of the TV set and my mother had Ed Sullivan on, and on came Elvis. I remember right from that time, I looked at her and I said, I wanna be just . . . like . . . that.

— Bruce Springsteen

While his appearances were conquering the uncharted waters of nationwide network television, his records were topping the charts in unprecedented fashion.

"Hound Dog/Don't Be Cruel" sold over 1 million copies in eighteen days and stayed number one for the rest of the year.

"Heartbreak Hotel," his first RCA single, made it to number one on all three charts — country and western, rhythm and blues, and pop — becoming the first record in history to do so and selling 8 million copies in six months. (A year later "All Shook Up" stayed on the *Billboard* Top 100 chart for thirty weeks — a record for a Presley single.)

A third of all RCA singles and six of their top twenty-five records were his. They were selling $75,000 worth—a day.

His first album remained number one on the *Billboard* charts for ten weeks, sold over 300,000 in the first month, and became RCA's first million-dollar album by a solo artist. Elvis also became the first RCA artist to have two songs in a row that sold a million copies each.

By the end of the year, RCA had to lease pressing plants from other labels to keep up with the demand for Elvis records. He had three gold records and was on the cover of *TV Guide,* featured in a three-part article.

Soon there was Elvis everything: bobby socks, sneakers, shoes, shorts, jeans (black, not blue), T-shirts, skirts, sweaters, blouses, necklaces, charm bracelets, rings, earrings, purses, ties, scarves, gloves, belts, hats, hankies, cologne, combs, pens, photo albums, diaries, bookends, dolls, guitars, greeting cards, bubble gum cards, party games, and lipstick.

At the end of 1956, *Variety,* the nation's venerated voice of everything entertaining, crowned Elvis Presley the King of rock and roll.

The King and the Colonel were already on to the next big

thing, but first, Parker had to take care of one small detail: June Juanico.

June was even prettier than Dixie Locke: dark-skinned, dark-haired, and truly beautiful. She and Elvis first met backstage in June 1955 after a concert in Biloxi, Mississippi. She went with him when he toured sometimes and visited him in Memphis.

When rumors surfaced that they were about to be engaged, Elvis, most likely at the Colonel's urging, appeared on radio interviews to deny it.

Elvis asked me to marry him, but there was no way. He was too hot and on the way up. Colonel Tom (Parker) never liked me: He didn't want me around too much. . . .

Colonel Parker was supposed to be Elvis's business manager but obviously he had control over his personal life, too. Elvis was twenty-one, and in my opinion old enough to make his own decisions. I was also of legal age, but his relationship with his manager was more like that of a son with his father. . . .

Elvis began telling me about his long conversation with the Colonel. He put an unlit cigar in his mouth and started to mimic his manager.

You're seeing too much of this girl from Biloxi. She's not good for you, son. You can't be linked to any one girl. Not if you want to make it in this business. Believe me, son, I know what I'm talking about. Don't get any ideas about marriage, either. And for God's sake, don't get her pregnant. You do and you're through, son, that's for sure.

— June Juanico

By 1956, the romance was over.

Just a few short months before, he had been the Memphis Flash, a truly local hero, and weeks before that a complete unknown.

Now he was a nationwide menace, a coast-to-coast, prime-time, multimedia sensation, and America's first superstar.

He had become ELVIS and he would never be able to get back to being Elvis Presley. Never.

ACT NATURALLY

They're gonna put me in the movies
They're gonna make a big star out of me
We'll make a film about a man that's sad and lonely
And all I gotta do is act naturally

Well I bet you I'm gonna be a big star
Might win an Oscar you can never tell
The movies gonna make me a big star
Because I can play the part so well

— The Beatles

Even more than becoming a famous singer, Elvis Presley dreamed of becoming a famous movie star.

When he was an usher at the Loews State he watched the movies over and over, observing carefully and critically the methods used by his favorite actors: Marlon Brando in *The Wild One,* and James Dean in *Rebel Without a Cause,* which he had seen so often, he could recite every one of Dean's lines.

Elvis tried to figure out just what it was that made them so good. One thing he knew: They didn't smile, and if he ever got the chance to be an actor, he wouldn't, either.

He spent hours in front of the mirror practicing not smiling, looking sullen, brooding, like he was smoldering inside — a volcano ready to explode just like Brando and Dean.

He believed that an acting career was more stable and had better long-term potential than singing. Who knew when this rock-and-roll thing might fade away, as it surely would. But, movies — hey, movies — had been around for a long, long time, and they were here to stay and so was he.

Singers come and go, but if you're a good actor, you can last a long time.

— Elvis Presley

Not only that, the Colonel agreed 100 percent. Make that 110 percent.

As a matter of fact, the Colonel was already on the case.

Hal Wallis, a big-deal movie producer (known to some as the Prince of Hollywood) became interested in the controversial new singing sensation when he saw him on the tube. He got in touch with Parker and arranged for Elvis to come to California for — are you ready for this? — a screen test.

In late March 1956, Elvis flew to the coast, where he had all sorts of plastic surgery: nose, skin — cheek implants, even. Wallis's instincts were miraculously confirmed: Yes, indeed, the boy had star power. The Prince of Hollywood offered up a one-picture deal with options for six more.

The Prince and Parker were a match made in hell. Neither one had any regard for, or interest in, Elvis Presley as a person or a real actor. They viewed him as a commodity to be exploited. Someone who could sell tickets, not speak lines.

His first picture, *Love Me Tender*, was a low-budget Civil War Western that was shot in twenty-nine days and starred no one important (or costly). It signaled to anyone who was paying attention (which didn't necessarily include Elvis himself) that he was going to become a serious actor only in his own mind.

Elvis liked the script, especially because it did not have any songs. That would change. The bad part was that he died in the end. That would change, too.

Once word got out about the ending, it was reshot. In the last scene a larger-than-life Elvis (taking up almost half the screen) was superimposed, singing "Love Me Tender" over the dead Elvis.

The studio made more prints of *Love Me Tender* than any movie in their history, and it opened in nearly six hundred theaters on the first day of release.

In New York City, two thousand people lined up in front of the Paramount Theater waiting for the first show at eight A.M.

Love Me Tender cost very little to make. So many of Elvis's new movie fans went to see it that it made back its production costs in three days.

By the time he made *Loving You*, the first movie written specifically for him and his first color movie, he had dyed his hair black (like Tony Curtis) and had his teeth fixed (just in case he had to smile).

Jailhouse Rock, in 1957, was easily his most interesting movie and best performance, although the critics remained, well, critical. *Time* magazine led the way. They said he looked like a sausage in *Love Me Tender,* and now they said his character was a slob, which was pretty much true.

The Colonel had cut a $450,000 three-picture deal (plus 50 percent of the net) with Wallis, and another lucrative deal with 20th Century Fox. That was for him and his boy. For just him there was his role as, quote, technical adviser, unquote. Since the Colonel didn't advise on anything, let alone anything technical, it was either blackmail or a payoff, take your pick.

Meanwhile, Elvis worked hard at being an actor. He took it seriously, even more seriously than the music, knowing that it didn't come quite as naturally.

The crew and the other actors liked him, much to their surprise. For *Love Me Tender* he had memorized not only his own lines but the entire script. He knew everyone's lines.

He was courteous, on time, respectful (almost too respectful with his "sirs" and "ma'ams"), agreeable to work with, intelligent, and not at all the prima donna they had expected. He was eager to improve. After all, there were plenty of good parts. "Meaty parts," they called them.

To make him feel more at home the cafeteria added burnt bacon and mashed potatoes with gravy to the menu.

There was even talk of a James Dean biopic after his life ended tragically in a 1955 car crash. Dean had made only three pictures, but what pictures, what performances. And now, here *he* was, just a couple of years later, about to become a big enough actor to maybe consider, just consider, the possibility of picking up where James Dean had so sadly left off.

It's a dream come true, you know . . . it's something I would never think would happen to me of all people . . . I had people ask me if I was gonna sing in the movies. I'm not, not as far as I know 'cause I took strictly an acting test. Actually I wouldn't care too much about singing in the movies.

— Elvis Presley

With the right roles and a few breaks from the critics, he might just make it. He just might become the actor he had dreamed of becoming.

But it was not to be that way.

Colonel Parker had dreamed a different dream.

GRACELAND

I'm going to Graceland
Graceland
In Memphis, Tennessee
I'm going to Graceland
Poor boys and pilgrims with families
And we are going to Graceland

— Paul Simon

That wasn't the only dream of Elvis's that wasn't coming true.

The new, nine-room ranch house he had bought on Audubon Drive — the one in nice, suburban Memphis — was becoming more of a nightmare than a dream.

The neighbors signed a petition complaining about the fans blocking the sidewalks, ignoring the "no parking" signs the police had put up, causing impossible traffic jams, playing their car radios too loud, and hanging around until dawn.

And that wasn't even the worst of it.

They didn't like Gladys hanging her wash out to dry or keeping chickens in the yard. And there were so many visiting relatives (who all looked, as far as they could tell, like hillbillies) that the place was starting to seem like a used-car lot.

The neighbors considered the Presleys to be lower class and tried to get rid of them by buying them out. Elvis got so mad, he sent someone around to buy up *their* houses.

When they had been dirt poor, people hadn't cared what they did with their wash or where they kept their chickens. Now that Elvis was rich and famous, they might as well be living in a fishbowl.

Elvis wanted Gladys and Vernon to look for a bigger place — something more private.

In early 1957 they found it: Graceland (named after a relative of the owner), a two-story, twenty-three-room converted church with a white-columned entrance, situated on thirteen-plus acres in rural Memphis.

Elvis paid $102,500, which was about $65,000 more than the other bidder. Once he saw how much his mother liked it, the money just didn't matter.

Elvis had the inside decorated with wall-to-wall wine-red carpeting, a fifteen-foot sofa and coffee table in the living room, lots of fake antique furniture, a king-size bed for his bedroom, and a fully functional soda fountain and jukebox in the finished basement.

There were blue and gold spotlights trained on the outside of the house so it glowed at night; stone lions for the entrance; a stone wall around the property; electronically operated front gates adorned with figures of himself playing the guitar; a pool; and a custom chicken coop for his mother's chickens.

At first Gladys was excited about Graceland. It sure had a lot more room than Audubon Drive but, even better, it had lots of privacy.

But somehow she never really felt comfortable there. During her frequent visits back to Tupelo she complained to family and friends that maybe all this stardom was turning out to be more trouble than it was worth. Not a blessing, but a curse.

She wished things could be the way they used to be. She never liked making changes, and life seemed to be much simpler before *all this.*

She wasn't exactly sure what she was supposed to do anymore.

They just won't let me lift a finger. There is so much help that I don't have a thing to do. I'd give about most anything in the world to live where we used to live; next door. And we could come sit on your porch. We could talk gossip, dip snuff, and put feed on your chickens.

— Gladys Presley

She felt trapped. She couldn't even go out to shop for groceries or take in a movie. She was overwhelmed by the sheer size of the place (the shack that Elvis was born in could fit in the living room) and felt like a prisoner in her own palace. "The Big House," the family called it when they came for a visit.

Her health and her relationship with Vernon had deteriorated over the years, and now, with the strain caused by all the new changes, things were getting worse. They had always fought, but now their fights were more frequent, louder, and violent.

Sometimes they fought because Vernon flirted with one of the semi-starlets Elvis brought home from Hollywood or with one of the pretty teenage girls who had become a permanent fixture at the Music Gates in front.

Once, Gladys lifted a pot of hot beans off the stove and hit Vernon right upside his fool head. On occasion he would hit her.

That's partly why Elvis called her every night when he was on the road. He was worried and wanted to protect her from his father: a burden no child should carry.

Of course all of it was made worse by the drinking. Gladys and Vernon had been drinking secretly (she ate chunks of onion to hide the smell) and not so secretly for years. Sixteen-ounce beers in brown paper bags and vodka for her, half-pints of whiskey for him. Some say she started drinking as far back as when Vernon was sent to prison.

It is also likely that Gladys used diet pills. Amphetamines by themselves can have a negative effect both physically and mentally, but in conjunction with alcohol, the damage can be deadly.

Elvis knew his mother was drinking even more lately. He could tell by the way she looked and the way she behaved.

Every time he returned from a tour or filming in Hollywood she looked worse. Yellow-skinned, coughing, bloated with swollen ankles, and vacant eyes — like there was no one inside.

She didn't even bother getting dressed in the morning, wearing the same housecoat all day, never going out, shuffling from room to room when she wasn't watching TV or lying in bed.

She was always anxious and real moody, happy one minute and sad the next. He asked why she seemed so tired all the time, but she brushed him off saying she was okay, although he knew she wasn't.

Making things easier for his mother was the most important thing in Elvis's life. He wanted to thank her for all she had done for him, working all those years so he could have a little something. Now he had money. That's what Graceland was all about — but it wasn't working out at all like he'd thought it would, and he didn't understand why.

Her son's success and the fame and fortune that came with it were making Gladys progressively more unhappy and nervous, not joyous and hopeful. Rather than celebrate that their financial woes were over forever and their future was filled with undreamed-of possibilities, rather than being proud of her son — the one with the nice voice who had made a success of himself — she withdrew into a cocoon of fear and trembling.

And then came the army.

Some believed it was no accident that Elvis Presley was drafted when he was, or that he was stationed outside the United States. There were powerful people who wanted him out of the way. After a couple of years in the army his fans would forget all about him. New stars were on the rise. Stars who weren't as threatening as this kid from Memphis. By the time he got out, no one would even remember his name.

And that's just what Elvis thought. Going into the army was going to ruin his career, he was sure of that. Elvis didn't want to go into the army, but he didn't see a good way out of it. Besides, the Colonel had already told him what to do.

It was a complicated situation, even for Parker, but the first thing he did was rule out any special treatment.

We can't have Elvis pull any favors. The country doesn't look favorably on boys who shirk their duty to the military. It'd be bad business in the long run.
— Colonel Tom Parker

Elvis wasn't going to entertain the troops like so many big stars had done in the past, although both the army and the navy would have welcomed that. And Parker didn't want him to weasel out on some phony medical condition.

Elvis was to say he wanted to be treated just the same as anyone else, and if drafted he would be proud to serve.

And, as always, Elvis did what the Colonel said.

Of course money was always the Colonel's bottom line — his only line, really.

He didn't want his boy performing for free (even if it was for the good of the country), because where would his cut be? A percentage of nothing is nothing. Asked jokingly how much Elvis's army salary was, the Colonel replied (not so jokingly), "I don't know. I don't get a commission on that."

Plus, maybe this thing was really a blessing in disguise. The Colonel could see it all clearly now. Who, after all, was better at taking lemons and making lemonade than a man who painted sparrows yellow and sold them as canaries?

Going into the army would help change Elvis's image into a more clean-cut, middle-American type that would broaden his fan base. He wouldn't have to depend on this insane rock-and-roll thing. Being in the army just might make him a more salable product, which, after all, was what he was. Like soap, or a vacuum cleaner.

And the Colonel was already turning out to be right. Elvis's patriotic posture was getting them some good press, and the boy hadn't even been put into a uniform yet. Maybe, his critics were saying, they had been way harsh with the guy. Maybe behind all the greased hair, the mascaraed eyes, the crazy clothes, and that god-awful way he moved, he was a right-thinking, God-fearing, flag-loving American just like them.

But there was one problem not even the Colonel could solve: Gladys.

Elvis was deeply concerned that his going overseas would be just too much heartache for his already overburdened mother to bear. She had been distraught since he'd gotten his draft notice and was dreading the day her boy would have to leave.

He wanted her to come with him and live nearby, somewhere off base. But Gladys wouldn't hear of it. She could just imagine what the Germans would think about the wash and the chickens.

He did manage to take her (and Vernon) with him to Fort Hood in Texas for basic training, renting a house off base for them in June 1958.

You could get permission to live off base if you had dependents, which usually meant kids, not parents, but Vernon and Gladys were Elvis's dependents, so he rented a three-bedroom house for them near Fort Hood.

Just weeks after moving to Texas, Gladys became ill and got worse by the day. She was so bad, she returned to Memphis and was taken by ambulance to the hospital. The doctors thought she was suffering from a liver ailment.

Elvis asked for emergency leave, but his request had to go through certain channels, which meant it was going to take forever. Elvis, in an uncharacteristic act of assertion, said he would go AWOL (absent without leave) if he didn't receive official permission pronto. The army was afraid it would appear that it was giving him special privileges, but finally, relented.

He went directly to the hospital and remained at his mother's bedside for two days until she insisted he go home and get some rest.

At 3:30 A.M. the next day, Elvis called and, although he got there in minutes, his mother was already dead.

Forty-six-year-old Gladys Presley died of heart failure caused by an acute case of hepatitis, surely aggravated by, if not brought on by, her drinking.

Elvis was inconsolable. He simply fell to pieces, crying uncontrollably, unable to comprehend or accept the sudden death of his beloved mother at such a young age.

Over and over, like a mantra, he repeated, "What am I gonna do?"

At the graveside after the funeral he had to be dragged back to the limousine.

Elvis had wanted her funeral to be at home, as is traditional in the South, but the Colonel would not have it. Elvis's manager was now telling him where to have his mother's funeral.

Elvis left instructions not to move or remove anything in his mother's room, and four days later was back at Fort Hood.

On Monday, September 22, 1958, after a lengthy press conference, he boarded a troopship bound for Bremen, Germany.

Elvis died the day he went into the army.
— John Lennon

PART TWO 1959–1977

AIN'T GOT YOU

I got a pound of caviar sitting home on ice
I got a fancy foreign car that rides like paradise
I got a hundred pretty women knockin' down my door
And folks wanna kiss me I ain't even seen before
I been around the world and all across the seven seas
Been paid a king's ransom for doin' what comes naturally
But I'm still the biggest fool honey this world ever knew
'Cause the only thing I ain't got baby I ain't got you

— Bruce Springsteen

He arrived in Germany lost, lonely, homesick, and fearful, although he never showed any of it publicly. His face was becoming a mask he hid behind — something that increasingly veiled his true feelings.

In a rare letter to a friend back home he did reveal the truth:

I would give almost anything to be home. You know it will be March 1960 before I return to the States. Man, I hate to think about it. Of course, don't say anything about it, because miracles may happen.

Boy, it will be great getting out. I will probably scream so loud they'll make me stay two or more years (ha). I can hardly wait to start singing, traveling and making movies, and above all seeing the old gang and old Graceland. All I do is sit and count the days.

— Elvis Presley

It wasn't quite all he did.

He dedicated himself to becoming a good soldier and one of the boys, and succeeded at both. He won a marksman and sharpshooter medal; participated in "war games" and maneuvers near the Swiss-German border; marched just like everyone else; and even earned his sergeant's stripes. He drove a Jeep, although most photographs show him atop a much sexier tank.

He surrounded himself with familiar people: his father and Dodger, his grandmother (who had promised Gladys she would always stay with Elvis); old friends like Red West and new ones like Joe Esposito and Lamar Fike. Lamar, who weighed in at 250-plus pounds, had hung around the Audubon Drive house so much, Elvis finally appointed him "court jester." They acted as bodyguards, business managers (along with Vernon), and companions, depending on the situation. Red spent a significant amount of time getting into fistfights in the local bars while Lamar made sure Elvis's shoes were properly spit-shined.

They all lived off base in an outrageously expensive three-story, five-bedroom house (The savvy landlady knew how to take advantage of her world-famous tenant.) A sign in German was posted outside: AUTOGRAPHS BETWEEN 7:30 AND 8:00 ONLY.

Elvis dated attractive German girls — some blond, some actresses; drove his new, white, two-seater BMW and enjoyed the nightclubs of Paris when he was on leave. He had his own hairdresser, dentist, and driver.

Then in September 1959, he met fourteen-year-old Priscilla Beaulieu.

Naturally, there are two versions of precisely how they met. In version one, Elvis's friend asks Priscilla if she would

like to meet the famous man. (Elvis didn't approach girls himself anymore — he had people do it for him.)

In version two, a less innocent, bold, and confident-beyond-her-years Priscilla initiates the meeting.

In either case, they met, and if it wasn't love at first sight, it was real close.

Priscilla had his first album and 45s of "Heartbreak Hotel" and "Hound Dog." She had seen him on television and in the movies (*Love Me Tender*) and had joined his fan club.

When she'd played "let's pretend," which hadn't been that many years ago, she'd always pretended she was going to marry Elvis Presley, and now here he was, only a half hour away, in Germany where her father had just been transferred.

Five-foot three-inch, violet-eyed Priscilla was vain (when a friend pushed her into a pool and got her hair wet, she never spoke to her again), extremely pretty, and quite sexy for a ninth-grade girl.

They saw each other nearly every night.

It was difficult to go anywhere, though. Once, they went to a movie, but there were hundreds of fans waiting when they got out.

Besides, Elvis was afraid that dating someone so young would get him some real negative publicity, so mostly they stayed at his place, listening to music and talking.

Elvis told her about missing his mother, worrying about his time in the army ruining his career, and how no one except for him took his acting serious.

And Priscilla told Elvis a story she had never told anyone.

The year before she had found baby pictures in the bottom of a trunk. Pictures she had never seen of herself being held by a man she didn't know. On the back her mother had written, "Mommy, Daddy, and Priscilla."

She was stunned when her mother confessed the truth. The man holding her was her birth father. He had been a navy pilot who died when his plane crashed on the way home to visit his wife and six-month-old daughter.

Priscilla's mother married her stepfather a couple of years later, and he adopted Priscilla but insisted that she never know. Priscilla agreed not to say anything to her stepfather about her discovery.

Priscilla's parents allowed her relationship with Elvis to develop despite her youth and the significant age difference. They were permissive about dating habits and were starstruck. The idea of their daughter dating Elvis Presley appealed to them greatly.

Elvis's enlistment was up soon, however, and it was time for him to go home. He promised Priscilla he would call, and she promised to write.

Although he wasn't taking Priscilla home with him, he was taking something else: drugs.

In the mid-1950s, it is likely that Elvis took amphetamines to help get him up for shows during those marathon touring days, probably borrowing some from his mother's stash of diet pills. It is also likely that he took sleeping pills to help him get to sleep — always a problem for him since his sleepwalking days as a little boy.

While in the army, Elvis began taking amphetamines more frequently. The drugs made him feel good: more self-assured, less insecure. Some said he acted more cocky and certainly was edgy, temperamental, and quick to anger.

He wasn't the same person he was two years ago. He hadn't died, but he had changed.

SAN ANDREAS FAULT

Go West
Paradise is there
You'll have all that you can eat
Of milk and honey over there

You'll be the brightest star
The world has ever seen
Sun-baked slender heroine
Of film and magazine . . .

You'll be the brightest light
The world has ever seen
The dizzy height of a jet-set life
You could never dream

— Natalie Merchant

Elvis's first national, post-army public performance was on TV in mid-May 1960. He appeared on *Frank Sinatra's Welcome Home Party for Elvis Presley.*

Sinatra had been the previous generation's Elvis Presley and remained a big star as he and his generation grew up (or at least grew older). He hadn't been shy about telling everyone how disgusting he thought rock and roll was:

> *Rock and roll is played and written for goons . . . [it] is the most brutal, ugly, degenerate, vicious form of expression — sly, lewd, in plain fact, dirty — a rancid-smelling aphrodisiac and the martial music of every sideburned delinquent on the face of the Earth.*
>
> — Frank Sinatra

Perhaps Ol' Blue Eyes was a little green-eyed, but he changed his mind fast now that his ratings were more rancid-smelling than Elvis's music, and Mr. Aphrodisiac had become Mr. Instant Ratings Boost.

The Colonel made Frank cough up $125,000 for three songs (approximately $13,000 a minute), the largest fee for a guest by anyone in the still young history of television. Elvis took to it like a duck to water, appearing newly coifed and tuxedoed. Just what the Colonel ordered: Elvis Sinatra.

The Colonel and his boy were clearly headed in a new direction, you could see that.

There's going to be a new Elvis, brand-new. I don't think he will go back to sideburns and ducktails. He's twenty-five now, and he has genuine adult appeal. I think he is going to surprise everyone and be more popular and more in demand than before.

— Colonel Thomas Parker

Gone was the frantic, rockin' rebel-with-or-without-a-cause, wearing the who-gives-a-damn-what-you-think clothes, and the greaseball 'do. This was the new, improved, smoother, slicker, sleeker, easy-listening Elvis. Elvis Lite. The one the Colonel (with his client's eager cooperation) had concocted.

It was like magic. He had gone from outrageous outsider to leisurely lounge singer in what appeared to be (because of his two years overseas and out of sight) the blink of an eye. One minute he's every parent's idea of hell on Earth, and the next he's changed into Mr. Clean-Cut, Wholesome Family Entertainment. The first true multimedia superstar with the accent on "multi" because that's where the multi bucks were.

Of course the Colonel always knew it would be this way. He had been pretty busy while his boy was over there keeping the world safe for democracy. It was no accident that there were plenty of articles and photos showing what a nice, patriotic, duty-loving, down-to-earth, and down-home boy Elvis was. No sir, no accident.

After the Sinatra show, Elvis and "The Boys" headed for the coast. (By now Elvis had "an entourage," which means people who went where he went and did everything for him, including light his little cigars and laugh at his jokes.) At this point The Boys included Red West and Lamar Fike; Joe Esposito and Charlie Hodge, both of whom Elvis had met in the army; and Alan Fortas and Marty Lacker, two boys from the 'hood.

The Coast. California. Los Angeles. L.A. Beverly Hills. But specifically Hollywood, where he was going to pick up his career but, unfortunately, not exactly where he left off.

Where he left off was *King Creole,* his fourth movie, which he finished only after the army gave him a sixty-day deferment before he shipped out. It was a well-written, well-directed movie with a respected and accomplished cast. Elvis gave his best performance of his young film career. Even *The New York Times* said he wasn't bad — high praise, coming from them.

King Creole showed that Elvis had talent, but talent didn't interest the Colonel, only money. The Colonel boasted that he didn't even read the scripts. He didn't care what they were about as long as there were enough songs for a sound track album.

The Colonel wanted Elvis singing in the movies, period. Once, when asked how he decided which script was the right one for his boy, Parker said he just counted the number of songs. That was it, plain and simple.

See, that was the Colonel's plan. Two for one. Not only could they pocket all that easy movie money but the movies could spawn sound tracks. They would promote each other. It was a beautiful thing.

And, if the truth be told, it was even better than that, although this part was kind of behind-the-scenes. It was better because all the songs were written by nobodies since the Colonel wouldn't let Elvis record a song unless the songwriter agreed to give them what amounted to, well, a kickback. But of course no one called it that.

So better songwriters just said "no thanks" and went on their creative way.

This left Elvis Presley, one of the great singers of the century, to record some of the worst songs in movie history. Songs that were profitable but not hummable or memorable.

Songs such as "There's No Room to Rhumba in a Sports Car," "Yoga Is as Yoga Does," "Song of the Shrimp," "Do the Clam," "Ito Eats," and "Queenie Wahine's Papaya."

G.I. Blues, his first post-army film, had no plot, no real writing, and no real dialogue. Just unreal-sounding sentences coming out of badly synched lips. It wasn't really a movie; it was a vehicle. An Elvis vehicle — or, more accurately, an Elvis Infomercial, selling the sound track.

They would do two or three movies a year, movies that would be made more quickly and cheaply than any movies in the history of film. One in summer, one at Easter, and one at Christmas. They'd fill them with incredibly bad songs, and the money would just come rolling in.

Under the Colonel's guidance, Elvis would become a fun-loving, easy-to-take, smiling-strumming-singing, happy jack kind of guy.

He would have G.A.A. Genuine Adult Appeal. Appeal that was wide enough that it could encompass every man, woman, and child on the planet.

But while Elvis was out there in the land of milk and honey making all this milk money and widening his appeal, there was still plenty of time to p-a-r-t-y.

At first Elvis and The Boys lived in a penthouse suite at the ritzy Beverly Wilshire Hotel — conveniently located in even ritzier Beverly Hills. But after a while they were asked to leave. Not because of the limos that seemed to be pulling up twenty-four hours a day filled with newly arriving Presley relatives from back East, but because there were, too many, well, let's just call them "incidents."

So one of The Boys was dispatched to find a nice place to

party. Elvis stayed away from the Hollywood scene — already becoming isolated from the world around him, whatever world it was. The Boys came up with a terrific house in Bel Air, an L.A. suburb. It was much better than the Beverly Wilshire, although there were some problems.

For instance, there was the problem with the Triumph motorcycles. Elvis bought nine, one for each of The Boys and him, and they roared in and out till the neighbors complained. Elvis had someone get a trailer so they could cart the bikes far enough away so they could be started without bothering anyone too much.

There was lots of time to spend dating nearly every woman who costarred with him and to play touch football with other celebs while the girls watched. Elvis's team always won, and Elvis was always the quarterback.

When he was finished filming, he and The Boys, with a little help from their amphetamine friends, drove back in Elvis's newly purchased Dodge motor home and, later, fully customized (to the max) double-decker Greyhound bus.

Back home.

To Graceland.

● ONCE IN A LIFETIME

And you may find yourself
Living in a shotgun shack
And you may find yourself
In another part of the world
And you may find yourself
Behind the wheel of a large automobile
And you may find yourself
In a beautiful house, with a beautiful wife
And you may ask yourself
Well, how did I get here?

— Talking Heads

Once in a lifetime, Elvis Presley did find himself living in a shotgun shack. But now, thanks to his enormous success and subsequent fame and fortune, he found himself living in a beautiful house: Graceland.

He had hoped it would be the gracious home his mother had always deserved but could never afford. Now, with her unexpectedly gone, it seemed empty and sad, so he tried to fill it up and make it happy.

He tried to create a Neverland where he, the boy who didn't want to grow up, could build his own world, insulated from the real world — a place from which he was growing increasingly unfamiliar and distant. A world where people would come and go at all hours. Where day would become night and night would become day, and where he would never be alone because there would always be The Boys.

The Boys from the 'hood, like Red West and his cousin Sonny; George Klein, president of Elvis's graduating class;

Marty Lacker and Alan Fortas; and his cousins Billy and Gene Smith. And newfound friends, like army buddies Joe Esposito and Charlie Hodge. Sometimes there were only five or six Boys, and sometimes three times that number. The more the merrier, and that included relatives.

For instance, there was Vernon — with his new wife. They had met in Germany, while Elvis was stationed there, and married in the summer of 1960. Elvis, deeply upset that his father had remarried so soon after his mother's death, did not attend the wedding. (He bought them a house nearby so he didn't have to see the new wife around Graceland.)

But he made Vernon his financial manager — an odd choice, since Vernon couldn't even hold down a job and knew absolutely zero about money matters. But Elvis figured he wouldn't steal from him, and apparently that was enough to qualify him for the job.

His father wasn't the only relative on the payroll. Other

kinfolk had suddenly discovered they had always wanted to be real close to him. In other words, they were looking for jobs and handouts, and Elvis willingly obliged. They became secretaries, guardians of the Graceland gates, and personal aides.

The Boys, meanwhile, took to dressing the part.

Sometimes they wore black suits, white shirts, narrow ties, and shades. Other times they wore identical hooded white sweatshirts or black jumpsuits that made them look like an out-of-shape SWAT team of sorts.

They all wore fourteen-karat-gold I.D. bracelets with

their names on them, and necklaces with lightning bolts and TCB, which meant "Taking Care of Business," which meant taking care of *Elvis*'s business, which was their *only* business.

There wasn't much of a salary, but there were lots of perks. Elvis helped them with the payments on their houses; slipped them a thousand here and a thousand there; bought them TVs, luxury cars, expensive jewelry, and other gifts.

Of course all expenses were paid for by Elvis, and that was the point, wasn't it? To live the life of Elvis. The swanky hotel suites, the huge Hollywood homes, the gorgeous girls, and the glitter.

Some of The Boys lived inside Graceland (a garage had been converted into an apartment) or in trailers parked on the hill behind the house.

Most had several duties: they were bodyguards, foremen,

and road managers. They took care of the incredible number of cars Elvis was accumulating and were his valets, running his errands and laughing at his jokes.

They would take care of him, and he would take care of them — that was the deal. That was the real job description. It was more like a cult than a job. The cult of Elvis.

And this was no nine-to-five job. The Boys were on call twenty-four hours a day, and Elvis's hours became their hours. When he slept they rested, because when he played they played.

The Graceland kitchen was open round the clock, and the cooks kept busy preparing the steaks and prime ribs just the way The Boys liked. (Elvis stuck to his favorites: peanut butter and banana on white, burgers, meat loaf, and mashed potatoes and gravy.)

They hung out in the basement shooting pool, playing records on the specially built record player, drinking milk shakes from the soda fountain, and competing for the girls Elvis didn't want.

When Elvis awoke — which was never before noon — he would come down the stairs and the laughter and the talking would stop, and the sound of billiard balls colliding would cease as everyone looked up and waited. Waited to see what kind of mood he was in: a good one or a bad one? Funny or serious? They had to know before they could decide what kind of mood *they* should be in.

The Boys would keep him company while he sat at the head of the table, drank his coffee, watched the tube (there were, at one point, fourteen TV sets at Graceland, and if Elvis was in a room, he liked it on), and ate his burnt bacon and hard-cooked eggs.

Elvis didn't like to hear bad news at most any time, but

never at breakfast, so he did most of the talking while they did most of the listening. But they were used to it; that was the way it was most of the time.

Elvis felt safe with The Boys — not necessarily close, but safe. Although he was surrounded by people, he was really alone. He was everyone's meal ticket, and everyone was using him in some way.

Nobody in this damn house likes me for myself. My own damn family only likes me because they see dollar signs.

— Elvis Presley

Of course, The Boys didn't just hang around Graceland all the time.

Sometimes Elvis would decide he wanted to see a movie. So he would rent the Memphian, a small theater fifteen minutes away. They usually arrived around midnight. Elvis and his date always sat in the twelfth row, where he had a table for his buttered popcorn, candy, Pepsi, and gum (and later, when one of The Boys made a run, his burgers and fries).

No one ever sat in front of him.

The Boys and their girlfriends and wives, the relatives, and assorted hangers-on, would all sit behind him.

There were always a number of first-run movies available because if Elvis didn't like a movie, he didn't waste time. He just had the projectionist take it off and put on a new one. If he liked a movie (some of his favorites were *Lawrence of Arabia, To Kill a Mockingbird, Village of the Damned, Dr. Strangelove,* and *A Shot in the Dark*) he would watch it three or four times in a row.

Sometimes they went to the movies every night for weeks

on end, but they didn't go to the movies all the time. Sometimes Elvis rented the entire Memphis Fairgrounds after hours. The management would close the park to the public, and ten or fifteen of Elvis's favorite rides would be turned over to him, his girlfriend, and The Boys.

Elvis controlled the rides, and they could stay on for as long as they liked — or, more accurately, for as long as *he* liked, which could be quite a while.

Elvis liked to climb out of the front seat of the roller coaster just as it was about to descend and scramble into one of the rear cars. Or just see who could stand up the longest with their arms outstretched.

They would have bumper-car wars that were so intense, girls were not allowed. They used pillows to cushion themselves and wore racing gloves to prevent blisters.

They rarely left before dawn.

Other nights, Elvis might rent the Rainbow Rollerdome, where the electric organ played skating tunes and the chili dogs and hoagies were on Elvis. They played a game called "The Whip." As many as forty skaters joined hands, formed a giant line rotating out from the center of the rink, and started whipping around and building up so much speed that at one point the person on the outside could be going as fast as thirty miles an hour before they lost their grip and flew over the guardrails.

The game ended when everyone had had it.

There was no end to the fun, though.

Elvis bought snowmobiles and, since there was little chance of snow in Memphis, had tires mounted in place of the skis. If he got tired of the snowmobiles, there was touch football, go-carts, custom-built golf carts, Roman-candle fireworks fights, and motorcycle racing.

After he was done making a film, Elvis had the Harleys

crated up in L.A. and carted back to Graceland. The obliging local police would shut down the highways late at night so that Elvis and The Boys could race undisturbed by traffic concerns.

Always there would be the Boys-Will-Be-Boys sense of humor:

We pulled some good pranks on the road. We'd stay in these motels and order room service. We always had more than one room. And sometimes the rooms were connected. So right after we hung up the phone, we'd start taking all the furniture out and put it in the other room and close the door.

The guy with room service would come up and knock on the door. And he'd wheel the cart in, and see that he'd come into an empty room. We'd be standing there. And everybody would act normal and keep a straight face. Nobody would laugh. And we'd watch the guy, and he'd look around. But he wouldn't know what to say because he didn't want to get in trouble with Elvis.

He didn't question it while he was in the room. He'd park the cart, and we'd sign the check, give him a tip, and he'd leave. Then he would go back and tell either the desk clerk or the manager. About fifteen minutes later, there would be a knock on the door. But between the time the waiter left and the manager came up, we'd put all the furniture back into the room.

So the manager would knock on the door, and he'd start off with, 'Mr. Presley, we have a problem. The waiter just came down and said all the furniture was missing in the room.'

We'd look at him like he was nuts. And then Elvis would say, 'What are you talking about? Come and have

*a look.' And the manager would step in and see that
everything was in place. And the guy's face would turn
beet red. He'd make some excuse and say he was terribly
sorry. And then, when he closed the door, we'd just fall on
the floor laughing.*

*We used to have a great time. The camaraderie then
was really great.*

— Marty Lacker

And if all of this wasn't enough fun, there were always
the drugs. So many different drugs that a makeup case with
lots of little drawers was needed to carry them around. So
many drugs that Elvis seriously considered buying a phar-
macy.

Like Elvis, The Boys (most of them, anyway) began to
live on amphetamines to get them up according to ET (Elvis
Time), and sleeping pills, sedatives, and tranquilizers to help
them get some much needed sleep when Elvis had had
enough. There were plenty of pills required and plenty of pills
available thanks to Elvis and his connections to the kindly dis-
posed doctors and pharmacists.

Elvis himself was becoming a real expert on drugs, constantly referring to his *PDR* (*Physicians' Desk Reference*). He
knew which drugs did what, how they interacted, how long
they took to work. He advised The Boys to drink coffee with
their amphetamines so the caffeine would help the speed get
into the bloodstream.

As a matter-of-fact, "speed" was the word. Things were
going so fast, nobody had much time to notice the changes. For
one thing, there was Elvis's temper. He seemed to lose it over
very little, with increasing frequency and out of the blue.

He got to smoking those stubby little cigars and if nobody didn't light it for him straight-away, he would sit there and he would seethe. Then finally he would blow up and yell, 'Am I going to sit here all day with this dry *@!%,$ in my mouth with nobody lighting it for me? If I am, then you can all get your asses out of here.'

It would be the same with a simple glass of water. The [empty] glass would be in front of him. He would stay quiet and then yell, 'Am I going to die of thirst or is some sonofabitch going to pour some water for me.'

At first man, man, we would only see flashes of those rages. But later on it was terrible. He would go into rages when things didn't go his way.

— Red West

There were signs. Some saw them, some didn't. Some said something to him (to no avail). Most didn't.

A MAN NEEDS A MAID

I was thinking that maybe I'd get a maid
Find a place nearby for her to stay.
Just someone to keep my house clean
Fix my meals and go away.
A maid. A man needs a maid.

— Neil Young

Priscilla wrote him almost every day, but Elvis never wrote and called only occasionally.

Then, one day, pretty much out of the blue — it had been months since they had talked — he called and asked her to come visit him. It's not exactly clear why he called. Perhaps he was bored and needed a new face, especially in light of his difficulties with his then current girlfriend, Anita Wood.

Elvis had been dating Anita since 1957, but by late 1961 she had given up on him and decided to say something:

We've been together for four and a half years and we just aren't going anywhere. I understand that Colonel Parker doesn't want you to get married, that I would be detrimental to your career and all that — but I'm getting older, I want a family and children. So I've made my decision.

— Anita Wood

Like Dixie Locke and June Juanico before her, Anita Wood had truly cared about Elvis, the real Elvis—the person, not the star. But he wouldn't or couldn't have a real relationship, and when it came down to it, he just wasn't there.

98

In June 1962, Priscilla flew from Germany to L.A. and stayed with Elvis for two weeks. He assured her parents that, of course, she would not be living with him, but that wasn't exactly true.

In late December of that same year, Priscilla flew to Memphis for a holiday visit.

Elvis celebrated, in rather dramatic fashion, by introducing seventeen-year-old Priscilla (he was twenty-eight) to his wonderful world of drugs. In fact, he convinced her to take such a powerful sedative the first night that she was completely unconscious for the next two days.

Elvis tried to convince her parents to let her stay, but he couldn't, and in early January 1963 she returned to Germany.

But Elvis (and Priscilla) didn't give up or let up, and three months later she and her father flew to L.A. Elvis, using his great powers of persuasion, succeeded in convincing Captain Beaulieu to allow Priscilla to come to Memphis to live.

Elvis promised she would live with and be properly chaperoned by Vernon, who was about as qualified to be a chaperon for a teenage girl as he was to be a financial adviser to a millionaire, and that she would be enrolled in a good Catholic school so she could complete her education.

Vernon's chaperoning duties didn't last long: about a week, and then Priscilla moved into Graceland. Either her parents never found out or they didn't care or both. In either case, they didn't say anything.

The Elvis Presley with whom Priscilla Beaulieu was living wasn't the same Elvis Presley she had met in Germany two years earlier. The one who was sweet, vulnerable, worried about his career, distraught over his mother's death. The one who told her his innermost thoughts. The one who needed her.

For one thing, there was always The Boys. He was surrounded by them (and assorted girls) constantly, so they were hardly ever alone.

She wasn't allowed to go anywhere without one of The Boys accompanying her. And she couldn't have any of her classmates from Immaculate Conception over to Graceland, because Elvis feared they would just be using her to get to him. She didn't even have her own money — she had to go to Vernon when she needed some.

The Boys, of course, resented her being there. Before she came, Elvis didn't like having the wives around — it kind of spoiled the party. But now that Priscilla was here, he wanted Graceland to appear less like a frat house and more like a home, so he eased up on the no-wives rule.

The Boys needed Priscilla like they needed a den mother.

Worse than The Boys, though, was the Complete and Total Elvis Makeover Program. He immediately and unrelentingly went about changing her from a pretty schoolgirl who wore blouses and skirts and fixed her hair in a ponytail into a Las Vegas showgirl.

He bought her thousands of dollars' worth of glitzy new clothes and, even though they almost always ate at Graceland, insisted she dress up for dinner. One night she wore pants, and he didn't speak to her for hours.

He had her dentist fill her cavities and cap her teeth; told her not to wrinkle her face, so it would stay nice and smooth; wouldn't let her eat tuna fish sandwiches because it gave her bad breath; and nearly had a fit when he saw that her nail polish was chipped.

There were evenings when he'd send me back upstairs to change clothes because my choice was 'dull,' 'unflattering,' or 'not dressy enough' for him. Even the

way I walked came under review; he told me to move
more slowly, and for a short while, he had me walking
around the house with a book on my head.

— Priscilla Presley

He had her hair dyed jet-black (just like his) and piled it in a beehive (a hairstyle fashionable in some circles) that was so high, one of The Boys said it looked like there were about eight people living in it. Then she sprayed it with so much stuff, it wouldn't move even if a tornado suddenly descended on the Memphis area.

Priscilla had always been a beautiful girl, but after being remodeled by Elvis, she looked, well, cheap. She wore lots of makeup — plenty of mascara and false eyelashes.

She had new clothes, a new hairdo, a new face, and felt and looked like a stranger in a strange land.

The few hours they spent alone were spent in Elvis's bedroom, which was a little difficult to adjust to. The heavy black drapes and the tinfoil-covered window kept it completely dark. The air conditioner was constantly turned to frigid.

They watched old movies and lots of TV, listened to gospel music, wrestled, had pillow fights, played hide-and-seek, and took drugs.

Now that Priscilla was no longer an amateur — not after her forty-eight-hour nod-a-thon — she agreed with Elvis that it would be a good idea if she took some speed to keep her nice and wired during the day just like him and The Boys.

In May 1963, Priscilla graduated from Immaculate Conception High School. Elvis didn't attend the ceremonies, but waited outside, so as to not cause a commotion. The school administrators were pleased, but Priscilla's classmates were disappointed.

As soon as the ceremonies were over, the girls ran outside (along with their parents and a few nuns), and Elvis courteously, as always, signed autographs. Priscilla's parents did not attend.

Then they went back to Graceland, where Elvis gave her a graduation party.

A few days later, Elvis and The Boys boarded his forty-foot Greyhound bus (new amenities included a queen-size bed, special seats, a lounge, three engines, and a lead sheet in the undercarriage to reduce engine noise). Priscilla begged him to let her go to Hollywood with him, but he insisted she stay at Graceland, possibly because of his latest costar.

Ann-Margret was a red-haired, sexy dancer-actress who was known as the female Elvis Presley. They were instantly and intensely attracted to each other and had a romantic relationship throughout the filming of *Viva Las Vegas* (and beyond).

It wasn't exactly a big secret. While Priscilla remained under semi-house arrest she read all about Elvis's dating his costar in the tabloids ("Will Elvis and Ann-Margret Wed?") and even the local papers ("It Looks Like Romance for Presley and Ann-Margret.").

Elvis and Ann-Margret, however, never progressed past the stage of passionate affair because Elvis could not accept her career. She was not willing to give it up for him. "Two egos, two careers — it didn't seem like a lasting thing. Women should be at home to raise a family. That's how I was raised. It's the only way to go," Elvis later said, referring to Ann-Margret.

He might have been a rebellious rock-and-roll singer in the fifties, but in real life, circa 1960, he was a conventional male who strongly believed in traditional gender roles. A woman's place was at home, and a man's place was out hunting for food or whatever it was he was hunting for.

ACT NATURALLY (PART II)

Well I hope you come and see me in the movies
Then I know that you will plainly see
The biggest fool that ever hit the big time
And all I gotta do is act naturally

— The Beatles

The twenty-seven post-army movies Elvis Presley made can be divided into three categories: bad, awful, and laughable.

Beginning with *G.I. Blues,* the early promise of the first four movies had vanished. In its place were formula films — fast-food Elvis movies produced with cookie-cutter sameness and mind-numbing emptiness.

IT'S FUN. IT'S GIRLS. IT'S SONGS. IT'S COLOR, the studio flyer declared proudly.

There were, along the way, lame and vain attempts to do some semi-serious pictures, but they didn't do nearly as well as the idiotic musicals (*G.I. Blues* and *Blue Hawaii* were the top-grossing films of 1960 and 1961), so idiotic musicals it would be.

It's hard to say what was worse: Elvis's acting, everyone else's acting, the scripts, the direction, or the sound tracks.

They gave new meaning to low budget. Besides Elvis's incredibly enormous salary, they cost next to nothing to produce. Interior scenes were shot on back lots, and costumes and sets that had been created for other pictures were reused.

So what if the music heard on the sound track couldn't possibly have been played by the assortment of instruments you were seeing on the stage? Or if the sound wasn't in sync with the action? Or if Elvis's lips moved and no words came out, or his lips didn't move and words did come out? What of it? Actors bumped into each other, dropped things accidentally, and the cameras just kept right on rolling.

They were done on such a tight schedule that scenes that should have been reshot weren't. Continuity was nice when it happened, but no big deal if it didn't.

In *Viva Las Vegas,* Elvis is wearing headphones and a baseball cap one minute, and is capless with headphones hanging around his neck the next. Ann-Margret, in another scene, wears high heels at the start of her dance number, but by the end she is inexplicably wearing ballet slippers.

Kissin' Cousins ("Elvis #14," as it was known to insiders) was a close runner-up to *Harum Scarum* for Worst Elvis Movie Ever. *Harum Scarum* was so bad, even the Colonel didn't like it. But *Kissin' Cousins* (which was shot in sixteen days, two less than *Harum Scarum*) reached a low point in its own right.

Elvis played a dual role as look-alike cousins, one in a blond wig. (How incredibly weird it must have been for Jesse Garon's surviving twin.) The stand-in who played blond cousin Elvis is seen throughout the movie only with his back to the camera or his face obviously and laughably obscured. Well, most of the time.

In one scene the stand-in is filmed accidentally facing the camera, clearly not Elvis, not the look-alike blond cousin, spoiling the entire (alleged) illusion of the movie.

Although it is obviously a gross error, the producer, proudly known as the "King of the Quickies," decided there was no need to reshoot because, hey, after all, this was an Elvis movie.

So who cared? His manager didn't, the producer didn't, the other actors didn't, he didn't, and, most important, the audience didn't. Thanks to Elvis's charm and charisma (he seemed to have more of both than anyone in entertainment history), his fans kept lining up at the box office.

A Presley picture is the only sure thing in show business.

— Hal Wallis

Wallis was right: No Elvis movie ever lost money.

It was all part of the Colonel's master plan — if the fans (read: suckers, in the Colonel's mind) wanted to see his boy, they had no choice. Their local movie theater was the only place they could see him. He didn't tour, he didn't appear anywhere, he didn't do commercials, or even give interviews.

And they didn't seem to mind that the movies had no real plots, no scripts to speak of, no decent dialogue, or competent directing. No content of any kind, really. Celluloid cotton candy. An "alternate universe," one film critic wrote.

Nor did they notice anything about Elvis's acting.

He seemed to have turned into a robot, sleepwalking through most of the scenes, clearly bored and looking like he was in a trance (which, thanks to his pills, much of the time he was), mumbling his lines without the slightest inflection or emotion, and bursting into song at the most unlikely times.

You can actually see him smirking to himself like he was privy to some kind of inside joke — only, what he didn't know was that, in the end, the joke would be on him.

What am I doing here? he seemed to be saying to himself, but the problem was that he wasn't saying it to anyone he should have been saying it to — people like Parker, Wallis, the directors, anyone. Instead, he said nothing, did nothing. Nothing to free himself from what he knew were deadly roles in dreadful movies and singing silly songs in even sillier movies.

If you could say Elvis was ever unhappy about something I think secretly he was very unhappy that he didn't get more of an opportunity to act. He wished they would give him the freedom to do other types of things.
— William Tuttle, makeup artist

He knew the movies were crap. Doing them actually made him sick. He hardly ever watched them himself, believing that he looked horrible.

Between 1960 and 1970, Elvis Presley averaged a movie every four months — an astonishing statistic that has never been equaled or approached (or, for that matter, attempted) by anyone else in film history.

Why did he let it happen? Why didn't he do anything? Why didn't he stand up for himself?

The Colonel had warned him from the start: Just do what they tell you to do, otherwise you'll lose it all. Now, he didn't think he had the right to say anything, even though he wasn't a kid anymore — nearly thirty. He was too weak, too passive, and too insecure. He could have put his foot down, insisted on better roles in better pictures, but he didn't.

Periodically he *was* offered roles that were, as they say, tailor-made for him and could have by themselves made his career. The lead in *West Side Story* and roles in such important films as *The Rainmaker, The Fugitive Kind, Midnight Cowboy, The Defiant Ones,* and later, when it was nearly too late, Barbra Streisand's remake of *A Star Is Born.*

But Parker turned them all down. Every one.

No matter how great the part or how much they wanted Elvis for it, Parker found a way to say no. Not enough money. Not a good role. Improper billing. Something. Anything.

For Parker, Elvis was a money machine, not an actor.

Elvis didn't set out to be a great actor making important films. He set out to entertain people, to have lots of fans, and make lots of money. He had that now, and he wasn't going to jeopardize it for anything.

I've had intellectuals tell me that I've got to progress as an actor, explore new horizons, take on new challenges, all that routine. I'd like to progress. But I'm smart enough to realize that you can't bite off more than you can chew in this racket. You can't go beyond your limitations. They want me to try an artistic picture. That's fine. Maybe I can pull that off someday. But not now. I've done eleven pictures and they've all made money. A certain type of audience likes me. I entertain them with what I'm doing. I'd be a fool to tamper with that kind of success.
— Elvis Presley

By "that kind of success," Elvis meant money: $1 million a picture plus 50 percent of the profits and this was forty years ago, when $1 million was worth $1 billion — well, almost.

A lot of people would (and do) do a lot of foolish things for that kind of money — Elvis Presley was no different. Although he was incredibly talented both as a singer and an actor, Elvis Presley always thought of himself, at bottom, as a dirt-poor southern boy whose bubble could burst at any time and he could find himself back in a two-room shotgun shack not just once in a lifetime, but twice.

But somewhere deep inside he must have been appalled, even though he said little publicly (especially after he got out of the army and the Colonel decided it was best that way). He clearly didn't want to sing in his movies. He wanted to act.

Here was the boy who dreamed of someday being the

next James Dean, appearing in movies he knew Dean would have laughed at.

And so, sadly, he let himself be guided by the "money talks" types like Wallis and Parker, who used him until he was all gone.

After his return from the Army in 1960, Elvis became a cartoon character. But he was not protected or given the careful dignity and respect Walt Disney reserved for a cartoon superstar like Mickey Mouse or even for an animated second banana like Donald Duck. Elvis was handled like Goofy, an expendable dummy who could be cloned and turned into whatever sort of dim-witted goon his masters demanded.

— Dave Marsh

He was the biggest fool to ever hit the big time.

Frustrated and bored to tears doing these movies, Elvis began to insulate himself even further from real life. He surrounded himself even more constantly with The Boys and tried to numb himself with pills. For a while it worked, but only for a while, because that's the way addiction is.

From the outside it looked like he was having fun, dating all those Hollywood starlets, while Priscilla, back at Graceland, took up modeling and dance until Elvis found out and put a stop to it. But Priscilla wasn't nearly as much fun as Hollywood with The Boys. They were just a wild and crazy bunch, having the time of their lives, weren't they?

Commuting between Memphis and L.A., getting some much needed and deserved R and R in Las Vegas or Palm Springs, or just shooting on location in Seattle, Honolulu, or

Florida. It was a tough job, but somebody had to do it. They lived with Elvis, partied with Elvis, played touch football with Elvis, had firecracker fights that lasted for days, water balloon fights on the set between takes (and sometimes during takes) with Elvis. Heck, they even acted with Elvis, appearing as extras and looking like they were lost. As if Elvis movies weren't bad enough, The Boys had to have cameos.

It was like he couldn't be without them even for a minute.

When one director had security escort the hysterical Boys off the set, Elvis threatened to walk and the director had to back down.

When he grew a beard for a role, so did they; and when he took his pills, most of them took theirs. Of course there were plenty of pills and plenty of excuses for taking them. There had always been the insomnia and getting up for the performances, and now there was the weight issue.

The amphetamines helped suppress Elvis's nearly insuppressible appetite for all things unhealthy and caloric. He needed to keep his weight down so he could look lean and mean up there, bigger than life on the silver screen.

Drugs, especially speed, were nothing new to the Hollywood scene. In many ways Elvis and The Boys were years ahead of the curve, and by the time they made the scene, there were plenty of studio Dr. Feelgoods around who were perfectly happy to provide him with whatever it was that made him feel good, although of course, that wasn't why he took them.

The pills, he explained to everyone, were completely and totally harmless. Not to worry. He knew exactly what he was doing. By now he was pretty much an expert — even knew them all by their medical names: Ethchlorynol (Placidyl); Oxycodone (Percodan); Hydromorphone hydrochloride (Dilaudid); Dextroamphetamine sulfate (Dexedrine); Methylphenidate (Ritalin). Of course the pills weren't recreational drugs like all the kids were taking. They were medicine; he took them for real illnesses and pain. Medicine, not drugs. He was in complete control, and everyone believed it, didn't they?

Of course The Boys had the best excuse of all: the boss. Taking pills with him made the boss happy, and that was what they were paid to do.

THE TIMES THEY ARE A-CHANGIN'

Come gather round people wherever you roam
And admit that the waters around you have grown
And accept it that soon you'll be drenched to the bone
If your time to you is worth saving
Then you better start swimmin' or you'll sink like a stone
For the times they are a-changin'

— Bob Dylan

The times were changing.

In 1960, John F. Kennedy became the youngest man ever elected president of the United States. The charismatic, handsome president and his pretty wife and young children (Caroline was four, and John, Jr., two months) symbolized the ascension of youth.

A new generation was taking over. A generation of ideas and ideals, of action and compassion, who would lead us into a brave new world.

Americans across the country shared a sense that they were participating in a momentous event. People felt good. Optimism was in fashion.

". . . ask not what your country can do for you; ask what you can do for your country," Kennedy said at his inauguration.

Coinciding with Kennedy's election was the rise of the civil rights movement and the beginning of America's ill-fated involvement in Vietnam.

Then, on November 22, 1963, Kennedy was assassinated in Dallas, Texas, and nothing was ever the same.

Music included.

It was changing, reflecting, and affecting the deep, profound, painful shifts taking place in society.

Since the summer of 1957, Dick Clark's *American Bandstand*, a daily daytime network TV show, had promoted cute, cuddly, clean-cut, teen idol types — Elvis wanna-bes.

Their songs invariably had a good beat and were always great to dance to, but they weren't about anything, really. Bubblegum music.

They filled a void. Much of rock and roll's true talents, due to scandal, legal problems, religious beliefs, and tragic accidents, were gone. The greatest loss being twenty-two-year-old Buddy Holly, who died in a plane crash and was immortalized in the song "The Day the Music Died." Rock and roll, it seemed, had lost its intensity and become yet another form of entertainment satisfying the ravenous American appetite for junk.

By 1965, however, two major influences had begun to dominate the music scene and change forever the way rock and roll was performed and perceived.

Bob Dylan, six years younger than Elvis Presley, was born in the Midwest and had his music roots in country, folk, blues, and early rock and roll, like Elvis, Little Richard, and Chuck Berry.

Dylan came to represent the singer-songwriter whose songs were personal, provocative, prophetic, and political. They were hard, not easy; complicated, not simple. They didn't have a good beat, and no one danced to them. You had to actually listen to the words or you wouldn't get it. Even their titles separated them from what had gone before: "Hard Rain's a Gonna Fall"; "Blowin' in the Wind"; "Masters of War"; "The Times They Are A-Changin'."

In 1965, no longer wearing blue jeans and a work shirt, Dylan stunned the musical world by blasphemously appearing onstage playing an electric (not acoustic) guitar and backed by an amplified rock-and-roll band at the Newport Folk Festival.

He then went on, without looking back, to record the best rock-and-roll songs ever, "Like a Rolling Stone," and countless timeless, priceless albums.

He elevated rock and roll to a place where the words were as important as the music. Songs were no longer songs but poems and political tracts. The music and Dylan's unique voice and uncanny phrasing added to their defiant power.

A year before Dylan went electric, on February 9, 1964 (only weeks after the Kennedy assassination), the Beatles, a British group named after Buddy Holly's Crickets, appeared on *The Ed Sullivan Show*.

Seventy-three million people tuned in. It was by far the largest audience in the history of television (and twice as many as had seen Elvis, although Elvis's appearance drew a higher percentage of potential regular viewers.) Not only had television greatly expanded its power in the intervening eight years, so had rock and roll.

Beatlemania had arrived.

"I Want to Hold Your Hand" (their first American release) and "She Loves You" were enormous hits. It is estimated that over half the singles sold in the United States in 1964 were Beatles records. *Meet the Beatles* was about to become the best-selling album in history, and *Sgt. Pepper's Lonely Hearts Club Band* (1967) further and permanently cemented the Beatles' deservedly exalted place alongside Elvis Presley and Bob Dylan.

In their wake came a renaissance in rock-and-roll music: the Animals, the Beach Boys, the Bee Gees, Buffalo Springfield, The Byrds, Cream, Creedence Clearwater Revival, Crosby, Stills, Nash and Young, the Dave Clark Five, Neil Diamond, the Doors, Gerry and the Pacemakers, Jimi Hendrix, the Jefferson Airplane, Jethro Tull, Janis Joplin, the Kinks, Led Zeppelin, Van Morrison, the Rolling Stones, Simon and Garfunkel, the Who, and the Yardbirds.

While all this was happening, the man both Dylan and the Beatles regarded as rock and roll's true trailblazer was no longer king of the record hill. By the mid-sixties Elvis's recording career was slipping, his music second-rate and inconsequential. However his loyal fans kept buying his abysmal sound track albums. *Blue Hawaii* was number one for twenty-one weeks and is still his best-selling album. But *Roustabout* (1965) would be his last number one for the next eight years.

The songs were so bad that the usually obedient and almost always hardworking Elvis started walking out of sessions, showing up late or not at all, and for eight months not even going into a recording studio.

It got so difficult to get him to record that the Colonel, never at a loss for ideas, simply used previously recorded songs for the *Tickle Me* sound track.

Since the sound tracks were making so much money (at least for a while), Parker didn't want Elvis to record anything new for RCA. If the suckers were going to go for the sound tracks, why bother with the studio albums?

RCA, boxed into a corner by the Colonel's sound track plan, just kept repackaging and reissuing old, second-rate stuff, further diminishing Elvis's musical stature.

His studio albums, although better than the sound tracks, were worlds removed from his Sun singles. The Sun sound was crude and intense, passionate and primal — almost otherworldly. The RCA albums are smooth, flat, overdone. Elvis had become a rhinestone cowboy when once he had been a white boy singing the blues.

Long gone were Scotty Moore and Bill Black (although Scotty still played on some sessions). While Elvis was making millions (by 1966, he was the largest single taxpayer in the United States and the highest paid entertainer on the planet), he refused — via the Colonel, of course — to increase Scotty's and Bill's $200 a week salary.

I figured the salary would get bigger as we went along. If he made more, we would be compensated more. I never begrudged him his success. In fact I told him that he should make more because he was the star, but I always figured I would share in it somehow.

— Scotty Moore

But there was nothing in writing.

Even as far back as *Jailhouse Rock,* Scotty had thought Elvis had lost interest in the music, and now it showed.

It all began with the material, the songs, which were almost always second-rate thanks to the Colonel.

Songwriters were not allowed to meet with Elvis or even speak to him about their songs. Top songwriters like *Jailhouse Rock*'s Leiber and Stoller refused to work with Elvis because of Parker's outrageous demands — demands he knew they wouldn't meet. (The Colonel once sent them a totally blank contract telling them to just sign it and he would fill in the details later.)

This meant that Elvis was always recording songs by lesser talent who were willing to take less money so that he and the Colonel could have more than their fair share.

It was the visionary Sam Phillips who had focused the ballad-singing young Elvis on raw rock and roll. Now, with no Sam Phillips, and only the Colonel guiding him toward the vast, tasteless American middle class, Elvis Presley was no longer even singing rock and roll, not really. It was mainstream pop, easy-listening Elvis.

The man who had revolutionized American music only a decade before had become musically irrelevant.

● DEEPER WELL

The sun burned hot, it burned my eyes
Burned so hot I thought I'd died
Thought I'd died and gone to Hell
Lookin' for the water from a deeper well

I went to the river but the river was dry
I fell to my knees and I looked to the sky

— Emmylou Harris

Bored with his music and movies, bored with The Boys and his life, Elvis looked around for something to fill the void. Of course there were always the pills. And spending money helped.

Elvis spent $500,000 in just six months decorating each of Graceland's twenty-three rooms in a different style.

Golden doors led to the bedroom where the walls were covered in black suede. The king-size bed, eight-by-eight feet, had a quilted black headboard, back rests, and arm rests. The adjoining bathroom featured a dark blue bathtub.

The furniture for the jungle room (so-called because of its distinctive decor) was picked out by Elvis and delivered that same day. His gold records were mounted in the trophy room.

There were mirrors covering entire walls; a mirrored dining room table; plush, wine-colored carpeting; and a custom-built fifteen-foot white sofa with an equally extra-long coffee table. One ceiling had hand-painted clouds for the daytime and little lights that twinkled like stars for the night.

There were two soda fountains, a pool table, a Jukebox, central air-conditioning, chandeliers, a gold grand piano, stained-glass peacocks, an indoor waterfall, an outdoor swimming pool, and gold and blue spotlights illuminating the entrance.

He renovated the barn to accommodate the horses, and then, seventeen horses later, bought a $437,000 (remember, this is 1967), 160-acre cattle ranch. And what ranch didn't need lots of pickup trucks and horse trailers (nearly $100,000 worth in one shot)?

Buying things for others helped. Constant gifts for The Boys (and don't forget the wives and the girlfriends). Donations to local and national charities. Cars for his secretaries, cooks, maids, and strangers.

Elvis had gone down to the automobile agency, and a lady by the name of Minnie Pearson was in there looking at cars, and it was pretty obvious that she was only looking, you know. And he walked over to her and said, 'Do you like that car?' And she said, 'Shoot, yeah, but there ain't no way.' And he said, 'Yeah, there is. 'Cause I just bought it for you.'

— Billy Smith

Eating helped, too.

He'd always had bad eating habits, but now they worsened: bacon; fried potatoes and mustard sandwiches; meatball subs; roasts; steaks; peanut butter sandwiches deep-fried in a whole stick of butter; Eskimo Pies; Fudgsicles; Nutty Buddys.

Sugar. Starch. Fat. Cholesterol.

Sometimes he would eat the same thing every night for a month. Sometimes he would insist on flying to a distant city just to satisfy a craving for a particular sandwich. Then, shocked to see how fat he was getting, he would go on one of his yo-yo diets: up and down, up and down.

He had studied karate while stationed in Germany, and now he took up kenpo and tae kwon do. He said he was interested in the spiritual as well as the physical aspect, but he spent a lot of time sustaining and causing minor injuries and breaking up lots of hotel furniture while demonstrating his prowess.

He became a high-degree black belt, although the true nature of his proficiency is questionable. Some degrees were "honorary," some he "skipped," and some were awarded because of money donated to his teacher to expand the school.

Then, in May 1964 (three months after the Beatles' appearance on *The Ed Sullivan Show*), Elvis met L.A. hairdresser Larry Geller.

Geller wasn't your average hairdresser. He introduced Elvis to the world of New Age spirituality: a world Elvis had been pondering. He brought him lots of books. Books on Christianity (including the Bible, which Elvis kept next to his bed, near his *Physicians' Desk Reference*), Buddhism, numerology, UFOs, parapsychology, and yoga.

Elvis read them eagerly, over and over, marking particular passages.

They talked for hours.

Elvis told Geller how empty he felt sometimes, how lonely he was. He talked to Geller like he hadn't talked to anyone since he'd first met Priscilla.

He believed that he had been chosen by God and he wanted to know why God had picked him and what his mission was. Larry Geller became Elvis's guide and guru on his new spiritual quest.

Elvis clearly had a Christ complex. He felt all his life that he was chosen, that he was a savior. He felt all his life he was put on earth to help humanity.

— Larry Geller

Elvis lectured The Boys, their wives, and girlfriends for hours, reading long passages aloud. He insisted that he could heal their wounds by simply laying his hands on the affected area. The Boys, of course, went along with it.

He read to Priscilla, who wasn't interested in the slightest — one of the rare instances where she and The Boys saw eye to eye. She, like them, was jealous of the time he was spending with Geller and worried about the effect it was having.

There was no more clowning around during filming because Elvis was spending so much of his free time reading.

At night he would lock himself in his bedroom for hours at a time, reading.

The Boys made fun of Geller. They weren't all that interested in God, spirituality, enlightenment, or any of that junk, and considered him a threat. They thought he was twisting Elvis's mind.

Elvis and Geller became so close that when he returned to Memphis from shooting a movie out on the Coast, he moved Geller and his family into a motel down the road from Graceland.

One day on a trip across the desert, Elvis had a divine revelation while looking at cloud formations. Exactly what occurred is somewhat debatable, since Elvis and The Boys were in their usual pill-altered state.

After the desert visions, Elvis read even more intensely. He told Geller he wanted to stop performing and become a monk. But after a while he became frustrated. He had read enough, studied enough, spent countless hours meditating, and still he hadn't attained enlightenment. When was he going to attain enlightenment? He wanted to know.

Then, in March 1967, Elvis tripped on an electrical cord in the bathroom and hit his head on the edge of the bathtub. Or so the story goes. Although there is no direct evidence that the fall was caused by the pills, it is doubtful that they helped.

He was unconscious for several hours and suffered a slight concussion. He had to rest for over a week before shooting *Clambake,* his next movie.

That was enough for the Colonel.

He had always loathed Geller and was deeply unhappy with his influence on Elvis. Parker insisted someone be with Geller while he cut Elvis's hair, to cut down on the conversation. But the bathroom fall convinced the Colonel that further measures were called for.

He dismissed Geller as Elvis stood by in silence.

Maybe now his boy would understand that he was a cash cow, not a sacred cow.

But getting rid of Geller wasn't going to solve the problem, and the Colonel knew it. He had to come up with something big, and by May 1967 he had decided just what that would be.

The King would take a Queen.

For over ten years, Parker had convinced Presley (who didn't need much convincing) that marrying anyone (Dixie Locke, June Juanico, Priscilla Beaulieu) might ruin his career.

Now, the Colonel decided, marriage might be just the ticket. It might "normalize" Elvis's private life (less time eating, taking drugs, and partying with The Boys). It might eliminate his constant concern that the media would begin reporting on his boy's relationship with a young girl. And best of all, it might be just the boost Elvis's sagging career needed.

Elvis and Priscilla had been engaged since December 1966 (due, in part, to pressure from Priscilla and her parents).

Having decided this was the way to go, the Colonel wasted no time. He made all the arrangements and didn't consult with Elvis and Priscilla about anything. From the Colonel's point of view it wasn't really a marriage. It was just another publicity stunt because, well, that's what life was, wasn't it, just a string of publicity stunts until the end, when he would have that big publicity stunt in the sky?

Everything was done in record time, and everyone who was invited was told at the last minute. There were no written invitations — only phone calls summoning the guests to Las Vegas, no reason given.

Remarkably, the Colonel purposely didn't invite most of

The Boys. Red West, Elvis's friend since their days back at Humes, took the insult hardest of all.

The Colonel had Elvis and Priscilla fly to Palm Springs first, and then, in Frank Sinatra's private jet, on to Las Vegas, where they registered under fake names to throw the media off the trail.

The wedding ceremony, with less than twenty people present, was held in a second-floor suite at the Alladin Hotel on May 1, 1967. (It is probably not a coincidence that Ann-Margret was also to be married in Las Vegas only one week later.)

Elvis sleepwalked through it, just like it was a scene from one of his movies. The wedding photos show Priscilla to be a little dazed, but even beneath all that extreme makeup she looks like someone who was finally getting what she wanted, but was wondering nonetheless.

Precisely nine months later, Lisa Marie Presley was born.

NOWHERE MAN

He's a real Nowhere Man, sitting in his Nowhere Land,
Making all his Nowhere plans for nobody
Nowhere Man please listen
You don't know what you're missing
Nowhere Man
The world is at your command

— The Beatles

In June 1968, Elvis began taping an NBC-TV special scheduled to air in November. Naturally, the Colonel figured it would be a Christmas show: Elvis would sing some songs, just enough to fill an album, and, well, you know the drill.

But Steve Binder, the show's creative, confident young director, didn't see it that way, and he didn't pull any punches. He told Elvis he was about to become a has-been, and this was his last chance to show that he was still the king of rock and roll, or at least why he once was.

The by-now thoroughly insulated Elvis wasn't used to hearing anyone talk to him like that, but Binder wasn't from Hollywood, one of The Boys, or working for Parker. Elvis wasn't his meal ticket, so he could speak his mind.

Elvis liked Binder. He could see that Binder respected him and was giving him a golden opportunity. But Parker (who purposely mispronounced Binder's name "Bindle") fought him every step of the way, constantly pushing for more Christmas songs.

One day Binder happened upon Elvis singing backstage with the other musicians. Informal music-making like this or when just hanging around Graceland seemed to be the only kind he enjoyed anymore. Taken with the relaxed atmosphere, Binder immediately saw it as a possible segment within the show. Maybe they could even film it right there, backstage.

The Colonel didn't think so.

Parker didn't scare Binder; he didn't give up on his idea. When the Colonel was around, Elvis didn't say anything, but as soon as they were alone he assured Binder he would do it.

Finally the Colonel gave in, but no shooting backstage. Binder could create the informal atmosphere onstage if he insisted.

Binder insisted.

Elvis asked Scotty Moore and D.J. Fontana (his original drummer) to join him. Maybe they could remind him of who he used to be before he'd become the Nowhere Man.

It would be his first appearance in front of a live audience in seven years, and he was nervous. He wanted to back out. But Binder prevailed. He was going on. He could walk off if he wanted to, but he was going on.

The audience surrounding the small boxing ring-style stage was so close, they could reach out and touch him. The handheld cameras borrowed from *NBC Sports* gave the segment an intimate, real-time look.

Elvis, who had lost weight, looked tanned and trim dressed in head-to-toe black leather.

Binder's vision was inspired, and he caught it all. The sparkling eyes that had charmed so many who knew him; the sly I-know-something-you-don't grin; the humor and the handsomeness that was still there underneath the dyed blue-black, lacquered hair and the extreme sideburns.

The movie star Elvis was gone, and the Sun Studios Elvis, the one who hadn't been seen since the army, miraculously appeared ("a resurrection," *Rolling Stone* magazine called it).

Fueled by stage fright, self-doubt, and the sheer joy of returning to live performance, he was startled and stunning. It was like the old days, right after they cut "That's All Right" and the Blue Moon Boys hit the road and Elvis would stride right up to the mike, grab it like he owned it, and sing like no one else had ever sung before.

Now he sounded like then.

Like he hadn't sounded in a decade: singing songs he obviously believed in, with musicians he felt a kinship with.

He joked with the audience (curling his lip and saying, "I got news for you, baby, I did twenty-nine pictures like that."); satirized himself singing "Are You Lonesome Tonight?"; told stories like the time in Jacksonville when all he could do was wiggle his pinkie; made insincere remarks about liking the new groups like the Beatles, which revealed his jealousy; and admitted that he was scared ("It's been a long time, baby.").

It was real, and it was honest.

Before the show aired, Elvis and Binder had a private screening. When it was over, Elvis turned to Binder and said, "Steve, I will never sing another song, act in another movie, or do anything I don't believe in from here on out."

"I hear you," Binder replied, "but I don't think you're strong enough to do that."

Sadly Binder was right. Elvis wasn't.

But for one brief moment on an otherwise typical network TV special there was the real Elvis Presley.

Seven months later, he recorded his best music since Sun: *From Elvis in Memphis,* which contained such first-rate songs as "Long Black Limousine," "Wearin' That Loved On Look," and "Gentle on My Mind." It was a critical and commercial success.

But then it was over and he was gone, back to being the Nowhere Man. This time he would never come back.

He had transformed himself into LASVEGASELVIS.

Elvis's first appearance in Las Vegas, back in 1956, wasn't one of the Colonel's better ideas. Or maybe the Colonel was just a little ahead of himself on that one. The middle-aged, middle-American crowd wasn't ready for the Memphis flash, and vice versa. Elvis was used to hordes of adoring, screaming teenage girls, not their vacationing parents.

But Elvis discovered something important during his stay. He discovered that Las Vegas was his kind of town. Las Vegas was nowhere, which was the best place to be if you didn't want to be anywhere.

The Colonel wasted no time parlaying Elvis's recent TV success into yet another million-dollar deal: four weeks, seven nights a week, two shows a night, $100,000 a week at Las Vegas's brand new International Hotel.

The night he opened, the two thousand-seat showroom (the city's biggest) was filled with celebs. The whole engagement was sold out. The 1970s crowd wasn't really that much different from the 1956 one, but Elvis was. He was no longer the rock-and-roll rebel. He was now a Vegas lounge act. Make that THE Vegas Lounge Act.

The International was thrilled. People were coming from all over the world to see Elvis Presley.

Las Vegas stage shows had never made money on their own. They were there to attract people to the hotel, which made its money in other areas. Other areas being gambling.

But Elvis was so big, he *did* make money. The first act in the Las Vegas hotel history to do that, with an attendance record unmatched to this day.

Elvis was money in the bank — *their* bank.

Everyone immediately signed a new, million-dollar-a-year, five-year contract.

The first year, Elvis was enthusiastic about the show. He appeared in specially made red-and-black karate gis and demonstrated his karate moves backed by a full band, a black girl group, and a white male gospel quartet.

By year two he was bored, and the more bored he became, the more elaborate the show and the outfits.

The karate gis gave way to bell-bottomed, bejeweled, and fringed jumpsuits in white and powder blue, complete with Napoleonic high collars (to hide what he thought was his too long neck), gold-lined capes that had their own names — The American Eagle, The Matador. Sometimes the whole deal weighed thirty pounds.

The shows opened to the stirring theme of Kubrick's

2001: A Space Odyssey to signify that this wasn't just a mortal performance: It was a divine appearance.

He talked to the audience sometimes at great length and sometimes incoherently. He threw dozens of scarves out into the audience (after they were hung briefly around his sweaty neck), or teddy bears if he was singing "Teddy Bear."

His singing began to resemble his acting: He was sleep-walking through it. Some shows were only eight songs long.

I took my wife to see him in Vegas in '73, we paid fourteen dollars a ticket, and he came out and sang for

twenty minutes. Then he fell down. Then he stood up and
sang a few more songs, then fell down again. Finally he
said, 'Well, shit, I might as well sing sitting as standing.'
So he squatted on the stage and asked the band what
song they wanted to do next, but before they could an-
swer he was complaining about the lights. 'They're too
bright,' he says. 'They hurt my eyes. Put 'em out or I don't
sing a note.' So they do. So me and my wife are sitting in
total blackness listening to this guy sing songs we knew
and loved, and I ain't just talking about his old goddam
songs, but he totally butchered all of 'em.

There began to be talk about his weight and how bad he looked. Elvis himself complained about his various ailments: laryngitis, bronchitis, the flu, pneumonia.

Words like "ludicrous," "depressing," and "tragic" began appearing in the reviews. And for the first time there were widespread rumors about the drugs.

The rumors were true. He was taking more drugs than he had in the past: Valium, Percodan, Demerol, Quaaludes, Tuinals, and others. His behavior onstage and off was frequently moody, short-tempered, irrational, and unpredictable.

In December 1970, after having an argument with Priscilla and Vernon about his spending, which was reportedly half a million each month at this point, Elvis—who hadn't been alone for a minute in over a decade, had carried no money, and didn't even know his own telephone number—boarded a commercial flight to Washington, D.C. using an alias. He checked into a hotel, flew to L.A. (another alias, another commercial flight), and then flew back to Washington and delivered, at 6:30 A.M. to a White House guard, a letter addressed to President Nixon. (The handwritten letter said he would like to meet with the president and talk about ways he could help fight the war on drugs.) Next, he went to FBI headquarters, but failed in his attempt to get a Federal Narcotics Bureau badge. (Collecting law enforcement badges and police paraphernalia, like police radios and revolving blue lights, as well as buying thousands of dollars' worth of various weapons, was a recent obsession.) He returned to his hotel, where a Nixon aide invited him to the White House, and he discussed the drug situation with the president.

Elvis had on his black suede suit, a white shirt with high collars that was open to below his chest, that big belt from the International Hotel with the gigantic gold buckle, and a lot of gold jewelry around his neck. And he topped the whole outfit off with this dark purple velvet cloak, and a cane, and amber-tinted sunglasses . . . he looked like Dracula. His hair was down over his collar in the back and his eyes looked like he was wearing heavy shadow and mascara. And he probably was. Above all, he looked completely stoned. . . .

When they were getting ready to take the formal pictures — and the White House photographer took twenty-eight separate shots — to kind of break the ice of standing there all stiff and posed, Nixon looked at Elvis and said, 'You dress kind of strange, don't you?' And Elvis told me he said, 'Well, Mr. President, you got your show, and I got mine.'

— Marty Lacker

Then the President gave Elvis the badge he wanted and he flew back to Memphis, mission accomplished.

• • •

Elvis wasn't the only one with a bad habit. By the time Elvis was appearing in Las Vegas, the Colonel's gambling habit had followed the time-honored tradition of turning into an addiction. He was considered one of the International Hotel's high rollers and, as Elvis's manager, enjoyed plenty of perks: a year-round office and three-room suite (even though Elvis appeared in Vegas only two months of the year), complimentary food and beverage, the entire staff at his beck and call twenty-four hours a day, and a $50,000 talent and publicity fee. Not only that, the hotel extended Parker a very generous line of credit (maybe even forgetting some of his debts — estimated as high as a million a month — from time to time) and allowed him to gamble by phone when he was away.

But the Colonel liked best to gamble in person.

He would enter the casino wearing baggy clothes and looking like a wrinkled rogue elephant. Walking down the aisles while hotel security guards cleared a path, he would point to the machines with his cane (he had a ruptured disk, caused no doubt by his three-hundred-plus pounds) while his underlings, carrying buckets of silver dollars, would shove them into the slots of the designated machines. He didn't even bother to stop long enough to see if he won, leaving that to the underlings who scooped up any winnings that came spitting out. That way he could continue unimpeded to his favorite tables: craps and roulette, where the real money was won. And lost.

Parker's arrangement with the International Hotel would later be called by a Tennessee court a "conflict of interest," meaning that Parker was lining his own pockets while screwing his client.

The issue of money was one that had been simmering for a while. Parker had been getting 25 percent of Elvis's earnings. A few stars paid their managers that much, but the industry standard was 10 to 15 percent. But the Colonel, gazing into his crystal ball, which told him that his boy wasn't going to make as much money in the future as he had in the past, believed there was only one thing to do: increase his share. Dominated and intimidated by the Colonel, as always, Elvis agreed to an unbelievable fifty-fifty split. But what preyed on his mind more than that was the Colonel's cozy relationship with the hotel. That's what caused the pot to boil over.

Elvis, a little out of his mind during one of his shows, had become irritated that one of his favorite hotel employees was going to be fired. He launched into a lengthy and unpleasant diatribe aimed at the hotel owners. These were Parker's pals, and the ones he owed all that money to.

This was too much for the Colonel.

After the show he followed his boy right into his dressing room and gave him a dressing down. The argument got heated and loud. Elvis yelled back, about the Colonel's gambling debts and how maybe they could get more money from competing hotels if Parker wasn't so beholden to the International.

The Colonel quit, or Elvis fired him, and then both threatened to call press conferences.

But the Colonel had been anticipating this day and had an ace up his ample sleeve. He would be happy to go, just as long as Elvis paid him the $5 million in outstanding expenses the Colonel calculated he owed him.

As always, the Colonel had the last word. Elvis, intimidated by the threatened $5 million bill, backed off, and things went on just as they had before.

The Colonel still had some rabbits in his hat. On January 14, 1973, Elvis's *Aloha from Hawaii* concert was broadcast live via satellite around the world. Or at least much of the world — forty countries — it wouldn't be shown in the United States until April. Over 1 billion people tuned in, which was more than the number of viewers who had watched the first man walk on the moon four years earlier.

Hawaii was chosen because of the Colonel's then-unknown illegal immigration status, which caused him to be afraid to step outside the United States. Also, Europe and Asia were potentially huge markets, and originating from Hawaii would allow the show to be on in prime time in Japan.

Once again, despite the problems he was having with his health, drugs, and appearance, the King's career appeared to be on a roll.

But his marriage was on the rocks.

TWO FACES

I met a girl and we ran away
I swore I'd make her happy every day
And how I made her cry
Two faces have I

Sometimes mister I feel sunny and wild
Lord I love to see my baby smile
The dark clouds come rolling by
Two faces have I

— Bruce Springsteen

Elvis hadn't wanted to get married to Dixie Locke, June Juanico, or Anita Wood, and he didn't want to get married to Priscilla Beaulieu. But the Colonel, figuring the time was right, career-wise, had insisted.

They went on vacation together: Palm Springs, Las Vegas, L.A., Hawaii, the Bahamas. They bought houses together: Beverly Hills, Palm Springs. And Priscilla decorated them, trying to make a house into a home.

Probably the best times were right after they were married, at the 160-acre Circle G cattle ranch that Elvis bought for nearly half a million dollars in 1967. They went riding and lived alone in their custom-built trailer, where Priscilla made breakfast and, briefly, they were a couple.

But it was brief. Most of the times they were accompanied by The Boys and their assorted wives and girlfriends. And, anyway, after a while, Elvis got bored with the ranch, and they had to sell off all the cattle, equipment, vehicles, and eventually, the ranch itself.

Even when they were at Graceland, where there were always so many people around, Priscilla tried to play the role of the proper wife, making sure everything was just like her husband wanted. But there was little chance to establish a normal, married relationship.

Elvis went out with other women the entire time he knew Priscilla. She didn't like it, but there wasn't much she could do.

It was as if Elvis didn't want a real life, only an artificial one. His life existed only on the screen, the stage, and the record. It seemed like he wanted it that way. Not only that, when they were alone they argued: about The Boys, Elvis's extravagant spending, his not standing up to Parker, and taking care of the baby.

When Priscilla was seven months' pregnant, Elvis had informed her that he thought it would be best if they had a trial separation. She had considered an abortion. Now that she was pregnant, she feared Elvis would find her unattractive — a mother, not a girlfriend. Her fears were well-founded. After Lisa Marie was born, Elvis withdrew, making her feel just the way she had feared.

Priscilla had no friends of her own, no life of her own. She became interested in the martial arts and took private lessons in L.A. and Memphis. By 1972, she was having an affair with Mike Stone, karate champion and one of her teachers. She and Elvis had met Stone a few years earlier.

When she told Elvis she was leaving, he was devastated.

After they were separated, Elvis tried to get Priscilla to change her mind and come back to him. He called her constantly and showered her with presents and told her she was making a mistake — it was their destiny to be together. But it was too late for that.

Elvis came to the October 1973 divorce hearings looking

bloated, tired, and vacant, even behind his now signature tinted aviator glasses. He wore a roomy warm-up suit to hide his weight.

Priscilla looked like a different person. Gone was the ridiculous beehive hairdo and the garish makeup Elvis had insisted on. She had always been a pretty girl, and now she was a pretty woman.

She hadn't seen Elvis in months and was stunned by his appearance.

The love that I had for him was truly love for him. I didn't leave him because I hated him; I left because I loved him. I wasn't about to see him go, in front of me. He had to help himself. He didn't choose to do that.

— Priscilla Presley

NOT DARK YET

Shadows are fallin'
And I've been here all day
It's too hot to sleep
Time is runnin' away
Feel like my soul has turned into steel
I've still got the scars that the sun didn't heal
There's not even room enough to be anywhere
It's not dark yet but it's getting there . . .
I was born here and I'll die against my will
I know it looks like I'm moving but I'm standing still
Every nerve in my body is so naked and numb
I can't even remember what it was I came here to get
    away from
Don't even hear the murmur of prayer
It's not dark yet but it's getting there

— Bob Dylan

In the fall of 1970, Elvis Presley took his Las Vegas act on the road. It was the first time he had been on tour since the 1950s.

The primary reason for the tour was money. His enormous and record-setting Las Vegas fees weren't enough. He no longer had a movie career, and his recording career wasn't what it used to be. Touring was his day job.

Despite the $100 million he had made, he still needed more. There were a number of reasons for this.

First was the decision to let his father handle the money without any outside professional advice. Vernon didn't make any good investments or any bad ones; he simply didn't make any. And his attitude about tax returns was even more foolish.

With false pride and misplaced patriotism, the two of them refused to take any tax deductions for the $20 million in charitable donations Elvis made. Not only were these deductions perfectly legal, they were perfectly ethical.

Each year Vernon allowed the Internal Revenue Service to notify him of the amount Elvis owed and he simply paid it. Getting caught forging that check nearly forty years before had had a profound effect on Vernon and his son.

Another factor was Parker: the obscene percentage he was taking, the deals he was making, and the deals he *wasn't* making. There were dubious deals like the one he had with the International Hotel and the new fifty-fifty split, but that wasn't nearly enough for the Colonel. He was well aware of Elvis's deteriorating condition (for some time now he had had spies within Elvis's inner circle) and he figured he had better get while the getting was good.

The Colonel concluded a major deal with RCA that served him well and seriously shortchanged his client. For one thing, Elvis's royalty rates were not nearly what they should have been or could have been. Not only that, Parker sold the rights to Elvis's back catalog — all of his recordings — for a onetime price that seemed like a lot at the time but, in the long run, cost Elvis millions.

Then there were the deals he *didn't* make, like turning down all offers for Elvis to appear outside the United States. He turned them down because he couldn't risk venturing out of the country, thanks to his then-unknown illegal immigration status. If the authorities found out, they might not let him back in. And he didn't want Elvis to go alone, because he could meet someone who might put a thought into his head. So he just said no, no matter how big the money.

And it was big.

Japan offered half a million dollars, the United Kingdom $2.5 million.

But the primary reason for Elvis's financial situation was Elvis's own ongoing expenses and extreme spending habits.

Maintaining Graceland was costly. Plus, there were other houses and expenses. The overhead, which included The Boys and the rest of Elvis's ever-growing entourage, his relatives, his divorce payments, and his new girlfriends.

He insisted on keeping a minimum of $1 million in his checking account at all times. He was spending money at such a rapid rate that, in 1974, when he earned $7 million, he still had to take $700,000 out of his savings just to get by.

He went on one spending spree after another:

- Eleven Cadillacs (some say fourteen) in one day (including one to a worthy bank teller he had just met); ten Mercedes-Benzes (including the biggest Mercedes stretch limo that had ever been made); dozens and dozens of other cars and motorcycles and other vehicles, foreign and domestic, custom and stock and all luxury.
- Thirty-two handguns, $20,000 worth at one pop.
- Jewelry. He had so much jewelry and gave so much away ($40,000 in diamonds given away to audience members in just one show) that he traveled with his own jeweler.
- Interest-free loans. His physician got $200,000 to start a chain of racketball courts.
- Flying his private plane from Memphis to Denver just to satisfy a craving for his favorite peanut butter sandwich.

- The planes made the biggest dent. Especially his favorite, a Delta airlines jet he had redone. Total cost: $2 million. It had luxury passenger seats for thirty-two, a bedroom with a queen size bed, a dining room that sat eight, a kitchen, lounge, conference room, wet bar, two bathrooms (one with a shower), four TVs, seven telephones; a $40,000-a-year pilot, a copilot, a flight engineer, and a stewardess. (You wouldn't expect The Boys to get their own stuff, would you?). He christened it the *Lisa Marie* and put a TCB lightning bolt on the tail.

It added up.

And up.

Initially, as always, Elvis was excited about the tour. Going from town to town, playing each night in front of a new, adoring audience, was where he had begun, and it felt good to go back there again. Nearly all his shows were standing-room-only, breaking attendance and receipt records. In May 1972, all four shows at New York City's Madison Square Garden were sold out immediately.

But the schedule was grueling. He played twice as many shows (mostly one-night stands) as other big rock acts, traveling to 130 cities and towns and playing 1,096 shows in seven years.

The Colonel was working him to death.

By 1973, after the *Aloha from Hawaii* special, he started to gain weight again. His weight would go up (thanks to his incredibly bad eating habits) and down (thanks to the amphetamines and the crash diets), but after a while it just went up.

And sometimes his shows were embarrassing.

Sometimes he was onstage for less than an hour, mumbling and stumbling through songs, starting them and not finishing, forgetting the words so that the backup singers had to sing most of the song.

Sometimes he talked a lot. Sometimes he was incoherent. And sometimes he didn't talk at all, just sang and left.

Once, he insulted one of the girl singers and she walked off the stage.

He was late and had to cancel shows, which he rarely had done in the past. There were times when he had to be hospitalized for "flu," "fatigue," or "exhaustion," but he always got up and went back out on the road.

He looked pale and tired, and was so stoned or sick (or both) that he could barely make it up to the stage. Once, he fell getting out of his limo. And when he did get onstage, he had to hold on to the mike stand in order to remain upright.

Concerts had to be delayed. Once, his plane had to make an emergency landing because he was having trouble breathing. Sometimes he couldn't go on until he had received "medical treatment" from Dr. Nichopoulos. Dr. Nick, as he was called, now traveled with Elvis as his personal physician. Dr. Nick would administer the incredible array of drugs that Elvis Presley now required just to sustain himself from day to day: Amytal, Quaaludes, Dexedrine, Biphetamine, Percodan, Dilaudid.

His woeful condition was the result of so many things both physical and psychological that it is almost impossible to isolate one from the other. The everyday grind of the tour was taking its toll. The endless traveling: on and off the planes, in and out of the limo, in and out of the hotel rooms. Night after night. Day after day.

Then there was "getting up" for each show, which was by now an ordeal. Drugs *had* to be taken because without them there was no show. The motivation and drive needed to be summoned up from somewhere, after all.

Some of his fans were shocked and others saddened by his appearance. There were a few boos and some left in the middle of Elvis's performances.

But most remained loyal — as they had for twenty years. They preferred to delude themselves. He just wasn't feeling well, that's all.

But rumors of drug-taking were finally being reported in the media.

The same media that was, by 1975, calling him "fat and forty."

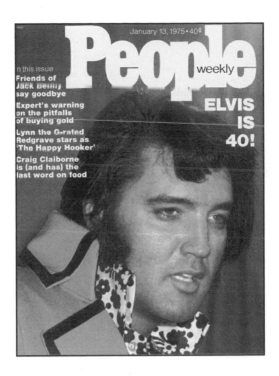

January 13, 1975 · 40¢

People weekly

n this issue
Friends of
Jack Benny
say goodbye

Expert's warning
on the pitfalls
of buying gold

Lynn the G-rated
Redgrave stars as
'The Happy Hooker'

Craig Claiborne
is (and has) the
last word on food

ELVIS
IS
40!

By 1976, the ever-vigilant Parker was booking Elvis into second- and third-tier cities and small venues. That way, the media might not cover it, and, because the fans in those towns had never had a chance to see Elvis, he could continue to "sell out."

In early 1977, Parker suggested that CBS film Elvis's concerts for a TV special. In the two appearances the footage was taken from, Elvis is shown at his most pathetic: grotesquely overweight, double-chinned, his pasty-white face mascara-stained, and his eyes half closed, as if he were trying not to be there. During one song he actually had to read the words from a piece of paper he held tentatively in his swollen hand.

It is difficult to understand, given Elvis's condition and the dubious nature of his performances, how even Parker, the King of Crass, could conceive of this. It is equally difficult to understand how Elvis could agree.

The only possible answer is, "Show me the money," and the CBS execs obliged.

Twenty-five years earlier, before he had become what one astute writer called a "public mute," Elvis Presley confessed to a Hollywood columnist:

> *I'll tell you one thing. I sometimes get lonely as hell. A lot of times I feel miserable, don't know whichaway to turn. Even though I'm surrounded with people, I get lonely and stare at the wall. I don't know which way to turn next.*
>
> — Elvis Presley

Throughout this period, Linda Thompson was Elvis's girlfriend. They met in the summer of 1972 (when his divorce was being finalized) at one of his late-night screenings. She was twenty-one.

Linda was good for Elvis and good to him. She was lots of fun (even The Boys liked her), and she cared for Lisa Marie during her visits. When Elvis played Las Vegas, went on tour, or returned to Graceland, Linda Thompson was with him. Like her predecessors, she tried to establish a genuine relationship. But Elvis continued to be unwilling and unable to participate.

By 1976, she was gone.

And so was he.

He had become increasingly moody, tense, dark, brooding, angry, and violent. Slamming doors, punching walls, breaking windows. He wanted Mike Stone assassinated. He shot down chandeliers and shot out TVs if someone he didn't like appeared. He accidentally shot Dr. Nick and Linda and pulled guns on people who worked for him and people who didn't.

There were dangerous incidents with outsiders. People got hurt, but it could have been worse than it was.

When he wasn't performing, he would fly home to Graceland and seclude himself in his darkened, freezing bedroom. There he would lie in bed, eating and watching, via closed-circuit TV, any of the rooms in the house and the fans who flocked to the Music Gates out front.

He would stay there for days, weeks, even a month at a time, nearly comatose from the increasingly larger doses of all kinds of drugs taken all kinds of ways: tranquilizers, sedatives, painkillers. Pills, liquids, orally, intravenously.

He just did these things because he could. There was no one to stop him, no one even to challenge him. He had not a friend in the world, which is all the incentive most people need to destroy themselves.

— Dave Marsh

I really get tired of being Elvis.

— Elvis Presley

Elvis Presley had grown seriously bored with his private life and just as seriously dissatisfied with his public career. This, combined with his inability to have any real relationships and his drug addiction, resulted in despondency and depression.

He retreated more and more into his own world, a world he was able to construct because of his enormous wealth, power, and fame.

He created a cocoon. He hoped it would protect him from the outside world. To a large extent, and to his great misfortune, it had. But it couldn't protect him from the emptiness and the loneliness. It couldn't protect him from himself.

It was not dark yet, but it was getting there.

TRYING TO GET TO HEAVEN

The air is getting hotter
There's a rumblin' in the skies
I've been wading through the high muddy water
With the heat rising in my eyes
Every day your memory grows dimmer
It doesn't haunt me like it did before
I've been walking through the middle of nowhere
Trying to get to heaven before they close the door . . .
Gonna sleep down in the parlor
And relive my dreams
I close my eyes and I wonder
If everything is as hollow as it seems
Some trains don't pull no gamblers
No midnight ramblers like they did before
I've been to sugar town
And I've shook the sugar down
Now I'm trying to get to heaven before they close the door

— Bob Dylan

In early August 1977, ten-year-old Lisa Marie came to Graceland for a visit. She and her father had seen each other regularly since the divorce: on her birthdays (except for the time
she was hospitalized with tonsillitis), or at Christmastime in
Las Vegas, where her father would introduce her to the audience (and where she met Michael Jackson when she was five).

Elvis spoiled "Buttonhead" (as he called her) when he
was married to her mother and now even more.

He had Elton John (her favorite) sing at her seventh
birthday, gave her a mink coat when she was nine, bought her

a customized powder-blue golf cart. Once he flew from Memphis to L.A., picked her up, and flew to Denver so she could see the snow fall.

This trip he had tried unsuccessfully to get her an advance copy of the new *Star Wars* movie, which hadn't been released yet. But he was able to rent the Libertyland Amusement Park for her.

Lisa Marie easily took to being the daughter of the King. By the time she was four, she was telling everyone she owned Graceland and threatening to tell her daddy if people didn't do what she wanted.

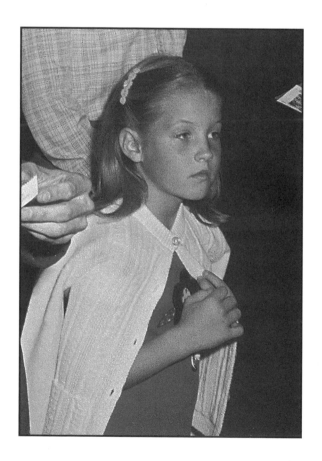

She was going to fly home on August 16, the day before her father had to be in Portland, Maine, for the first stop on his upcoming tour.

Only days earlier, *Elvis: What Happened?*, a book written by Red West, his cousin Sonny West, and Dave Hebler, another one of Elvis's bodyguards, was published. The book was a result of something that had happened a year earlier.

Vernon and Elvis had agreed to downsize, and Vernon had decided a good place to start would be with Red, Sonny, and Dave Hebler. He called them up, told them they were fired due to cost, and gave them a week's pay. Elvis hadn't bothered to speak to any of them. Not even Red, who had been his friend for twenty-five years.

Money *was* part of it. A number of lawsuits had been brought against Elvis recently by people who claimed that they had been beaten up by his bodyguards.

A month later there were rumors that the three of them were planning to write a book — rumors that Elvis became aware of. He hired a private investigator to find out what was going to be in the book and to offer them money not to do it.

They turned down the offer.

Elvis felt betrayed by the three and became obsessed and fearful about the book. He knew it would reveal, for the first time, some of the less wonderful things about his private life. And there was nothing Red didn't know.

On August 4, 1977, *Elvis: What Happened?* was published. Elvis was horrified and certain it was going to destroy his reputation and his career.

August 14 was the anniversary of his mother's death — always a painful day.

On August 15, Dr. Nick ordered the drugs that would be

needed for the upcoming tour. The luggage was packed and in the hallway, waiting to be taken to the plane.

At about ten-thirty that night, Elvis went to visit his dentist (going to the dentist at that hour was not unusual for Elvis). After that, accompanied by Ginger Alden, former Memphis Miss Traffic Safety, and others, he watched a movie.

Then he played racquetball (Dr. Nick's idea of helping Elvis keep in shape — he weighed 250 pounds now) until four in the morning. Then he and Ginger went to his bedroom, and as he frequently did, Elvis went into the bathroom to read while Ginger went to sleep.

At one o'clock the next afternoon, Ginger Alden found him lying facedown on the bathroom floor. All attempts to revive him failed, and on Tuesday, August 16, 1977, forty-two-year-old Elvis Presley was pronounced dead on arrival at Baptist Memorial Hospital.

Hospital officials, reporting on the preliminary autopsy, stated that he had died of cardiac arrhythmia and that there was no evidence of drug abuse. He died, they said, a natural death.

These findings have been contested over the years, and it is now believed that Elvis Presley died of polypharmacy: the lethal interaction of a number of drugs.

The record we have, Doctor — and I'll say this as gently as I possibly can — indicate that from January 20, 1977 until August 16, 1977, the day he died, you prescribed to Elvis Presley, and the prescriptions were all signed by you — over five thousand schedule two narcotics and/or amphetamines. This comes to something like twenty, twenty-five per day.

— ABC News interview of Dr. Nichopoulos

Some, citing his continued anguish over his divorce, his age and condition, the publication of *Elvis: What Happened?*, and the anniversary of his mother's death, believe Elvis Presley purposely took an overdose.

On August 17, over fifty thousand people lined up at Graceland to pay their respects.

The funeral, on August 18, was the busiest day in FTD history. An extra five tons of flowers were flown in to fill the orders for the two thousand floral arrangements.

Parker attended the funeral dressed in a Hawaiian sport shirt (some insist it was a plain blue one) and a baseball cap, and refused to be a pallbearer or take part in the funeral at all. Throughout, he sat off by himself, leaning on a police motorcycle.

"A Lonely Life Ends on Elvis Presley Boulevard" read a Memphis newspaper headline.

Elvis Presley was eventually buried next to his mother in the meditation garden he created on the grounds of Graceland.

● CHRONOLOGY

January 8, 1935. Elvis Aron Presley born, East Tupelo, Mississippi.

November 1948. Family moves to Memphis, Tennessee.

June 1953. Graduates from Humes High School.

Summer 1953. Records first acetate, Memphis Recording Service.

July 1954. Releases first record.

August 1955. Signs management contract with Colonel Thomas A. Parker.

November 1955. Signs recording contract with RCA.

January 1956. Releases the single "Heartbreak Hotel."
    First network TV appearance.

March 1956. Releases first album.

April 1956. Signs movie contract.
    "Heartbreak Hotel" becomes Elvis's first gold record.

September 1956. First appearance on *The Ed Sullivan Show*.

November 1956. Releases "Love Me Tender."

March 1957. Buys Graceland.

March 1958. Inducted into the army.

August 14, 1958. Gladys Presley dies.

September 1959. Meets Priscilla Beaulieu.

March 1960. Discharged from army.

May 1960. Appears on *Frank Sinatra's Welcome Home Party for Elvis Presley*.

March 1963. Priscilla Beaulieu arrives in the United States.

February 9, 1964. The Beatles appear on *The Ed Sullivan Show*.

June 1965. Bob Dylan appears at Newport Folk Festival.

May 1, 1967. Marries Priscilla Beaulieu.

February 1, 1968. Lisa Marie Presley born.

December 3, 1968. *Elvis* TV special broadcast.

July 1969. Opens at International Hotel, Las Vegas.

March 1970. Five gold records.

December 1970. Meets with President Richard M. Nixon.

June 1972. Appears at Madison Square Garden, New York City.

January 1973. *Aloha from Hawaii* broadcast.

October 1973. Divorces Priscilla Presley.

August 16, 1977. Dies.

● BIBLIOGRAPHY

Bane, Michael. *White Boy Singin' the Blues: The Black Roots of White Rock*. New York: Da Capo Press, 1982.

Bova, Joyce. *Don't Ask Forever: My Love Affair with Elvis*. New York: Kensington, 1994.

Brown, Peter Harry, and Pat H. Broeske. *Down at the End of Lonely Street*. New York: Penguin Putnam Inc., 1997.

Burk, Bill E. *Early Elvis: The Sun Years*. Memphis, TN: Propwash, 1997.

Choron, Sandra, and Bob Oskam. *Elvis! The Last Word*. New York: Citadel Press, 1991.

Coffey, Frank. *The Complete Idiot's Guide to Elvis*. New York: Alpha Books, 1997.

Cohn, Nik. *Rock: From the Beginning*. New York: Pocket Books, 1970.

Cotten, Lee. *All Shook Up: Elvis Day-By-Day 1954–1977*. Ann Arbor, MI: Popular Culture, Ink., 1998.

Crumbaker, Marge, with Gabe Tucker. *Up & Down with Elvis Presley: The Inside Story*. New York: G. P. Putnam's Sons, 1981.

Curtin, Jim. *Unseen Elvis: Candids of the King*. Boston: Bulfinch/ Little, Brown, 1992.

———. *Elvis: Unknown Stories Behind the Legend*. Nashville: Celebrity Books, 1998.

DeCurtis, Anthony, and James Henke. *The Rolling Stone Illustrated History of Rock & Roll*. New York: Random House, 1992.

Doss, Erika. *Elvis Culture: Fans, Faith & Image*. Lawrence: University Press of Kansas, 1999.

Dundy, Elaine. *Elvis and Gladys: The Genesis of the King*. London: Futura, 1985.

Escott, Colin, with Martin Hawkins. *Good Rockin's Rockin' Tonight: Sun Records and the Birth of Rock and Roll*. New York: St. Martin's Press, 1992.

Finstad, Suzanne. *Child Bride*. New York: Berkeley, 1997.

Fortas, Alan. *Elvis: From Memphis to Hollywood*. Ann Arbor, MI: Popular Culture, Ink., 1992.

Geller, Larry. *"If I Can Dream": Elvis' Own Story*. New York: Simon and Schuster, 1989.

Gillett, Charlie. *The Sound of the City: The Rise of Rock and Roll*. New York: Da Capo Press, 1996.

Gilmore, Mikal. *Night Beat: A Shadow History of Rock and Roll*. New York: Anchor Books, 1998.

Goldman, Alber. *Elvis*. New York: McGraw-Hill, 1981.

——. *Elvis: The Last 24 Hours*. New York: St. Martin's Press, 1991.

Gray, Michael, and Roger Osborne. *The Elvis Atlas: A Journey Through Elvis Presley's America*. New York: Henry Holt and Company, 1996.

Greenwood, Earl, and Kathleen Tracy. *The Boy Who Would Be King*. New York: Dutton, 1990.

Gregory, James, ed. *The Elvis Presley Story*. New York: Hillman, 1960.

Gregory, Neal, and Janice Gregory. *When Elvis Died*. New York: Pharos, 1980.

Grossman, Loyd. *A Social History of Rock Music*. New York: David McKay, 1976.

Guernsey's. *Elvis Presley: The Official Auction Featuring Items from the Archives of Graceland*. New York: Harry N. Abrams, Inc., 1999.

Guralnick, Peter. *Careless Love: The Unmaking of Elvis Presley*. Boston: Little, Brown, 1999.

————. *Last Train to Memphis: The Rise of Elvis Presley*. Boston: Little, Brown, 1995.

————. *Lost Highway: Journeys and Arrivals of American Musicians*. Boston: Little, Brown, 1999.

Guralnick, Peter, and Ernst Jorgensen. *Elvis Day By Day*. New York: Ballantine Books, 1999.

Haining, Peter, ed. *Elvis in Private*. New York: St. Martin's Press, 1987.

Halberstam, David. *The Fifties*. New York: Villard, 1993.

Harrison, Ted. *Elvis People: The Cult of the King*. London: Fount, 1992.

Hazen, Cindy, and Mike Freeman. *Memphis Elvis Style*. Winston-Salem, NC: John F. Blair, 1997.

Hinds, Mary Hancock. *Infinite Elvis: An Annotated Bibliography*. Chicago: A Capella Books, 2001.

Hopkins, Jerry. *Elvis: A Biography*. London: Open Gate, 1971.

———. *Elvis: The Final Years*. New York: Playboy Paperbacks, 1981.

Jackson, John A. *Big Beat Heat: Alan Freed and the Early Years of Rock & Roll*. New York: Schirmer Books, 1991.

Jorgensen, Ernst. *Elvis Presley: A Life in Music. The Complete Recording Sessions*. New York: St. Martin's Press, 1998.

Juanico, June. *Elvis: In the Twilight of Memory*. New York: Arcade, 1997.

Lacker, Marty, Patsy Lacker, and Leslie S. Smith. *Elvis: Portrait of a Friend*. Memphis, TN: Wimmer Brothers Books, 1970.

Landau, Jon. *It's Too Late to Stop Now: A Rock and Roll Journal*. San Francisco: Straight Arrow, 1972.

Lichter, Paul. *The Boy Who Dared to Rock: The Definitive Elvis*. Garden City, NY: Dolphin Books, 1978.

Marcus, Greil. *Dead Elvis: A Chronicle of a Cultural Obsession*. Cambridge: Harvard University Press, 1991.

———. *Invisible Republic: Bob Dylan's Basement Tapes*. New York: Henry Holt, 1997.

———. *Mystery Train: Images of America in Rock 'N' Roll Music*. New York: Plume, 1997.

———. *Double Trouble: Bill Clinton and Elvis Presley in a Land of No Alternatives*. New York: Henry Holt, 2000.

Marling, Karal Ann. *As Seen on TV: The Visual Clutter of Everyday Life in the 1950's*. Cambridge: Harvard University Press, 1994.

———. *Graceland: Going Home with Elvis*. Cambridge: Harvard University Press, 1996.

Marsh, Dave. *Elvis*. New York: Thunder Mouth Press, 1992.

Miller, James. *Flowers in the Dustbin: The Rise of Rock and Roll, 1947–1977*. New York: Simon and Schuster, 1999.

Moore, Scotty. *That's Alright, Elvis*. New York: Schirmer Books, 1997.

O'Neal, Sean. *Elvis Inc.: The Fall and Rise of the Presley Empire*. Rocklin: Prima, 1996.

———. *My Boy Elvis: The Colonel Tom Parker Story*. New York: Barricade, 1998.

Osborne, Jerry. *Elvis Word for Word*. New York: Harmony Books, 1999.

Physicians' Desk Reference. Montvale, NJ: Medical Economics Co., 2000.

Pond, Steve. *Elvis in Hollywood*. New York: New American Library, 1990.

Presley, Priscilla Beaulieu. *Elvis and Me*. New York: Berkeley, 1986.

Quain, Kevin. *The Elvis Reader*. New York: St. Martin's Press, 1992.

Roy, Samuel, and Tom Aspell. *The Essential Elvis*. Nashville, TN: Rutledge Hill Press, 1998.

Schroer, Andreas. *Private Presley: The Missing Years — Elvis in Germany*. New York: William Morrow, 1993.

Smith, Gene. *Elvis's Man Friday*. Nashville, TN: Light of Day Publishing, 1994.

Stanley, Billy. *Elvis My Brother: An Intimate Family Memoir of Life with the King*. New York: St. Martin's Press, 1989.

Staten, Vince. *The Real Elvis: Good Old Boy*. Dayton, OH: Media Ventures, Inc., 1978.

Stearn, Jess, with Larry Geller. *The Truth About Elvis*. New York: Jove, 1980.

Stern, Jane, and Michael Stern. *Elvis World*. New York: Knopf, 1987.

Strausbaugh, John. *Reflections on the Birth of Elvis Faith*. New York: Blast Books, 1995.

Tharpe, Jac L. *Elvis: Images and Fancies*. Jackson: University Press of Mississippi, 1979.

Tosches, Nick. *Country: The Twisted Roots of Rock 'N' Roll*. New York: Da Capo, 1985.

Vellenga, Dirk, with Mick Farren. *Elvis and the Colonel*. New York: Delacorte, 1981.

Wertheimer, Alfred. *Elvis '56: In the Beginning*. New York: Pimlico, 1994.

West, Red, Sonny West, and Dave Hebler. *Elvis: What Happened?* New York: Ballantine Books, 1977.

Whitmer, Peter. *The Inner Elvis*. New York: Hyperion, 1996.

Worth, Fred L., and Steve Tamerius. *Elvis: His Life from A to Z*. New York: Wings Books, 1990.

Yancey, Becky, with Cliff Linedecker. *My Life with Elvis*. New York: St. Martin's Press, 1977.

Zmijewsky, Steven, and Boris Zmijewsky. *The Films and Career of Elvis*. New York: Citadel Press, 1991.

● VIDEOGRAPHY

Elvis: Aloha from Hawaii (Lightyear, 1990)

Elvis: '68 Comeback Special (Lightyear, 1968)

Elvis: All the King's Men (Real Entertainment, 1997)

Elvis: August 7, 1955 (Monty Robertson Enterprises, 1998)

Elvis: The Beginning 1954/1955 (Elvis Presley Enterprises, 1993)

Elvis: The Complete Story (Passport Video, 1997)

Elvis: Death of a Legend (Dan Dalton Productions, 1997)

Elvis: The Echo Will Never Die (Four Point Entertainment, 1986)

Elvis: The Great Performances (The Elvis Presley Estate, 1989)

Elvis: The Lost Performances (MGM/UA, 1992)

Elvis: One Night with You (Lightyear, 1985)

Elvis: Story of a Legend (A&E Home Video, 1993)

Elvis: That's the Way It Is (MGM/UA, 1970)

He Touched Me: The Gospel Music of Elvis Presley (Coming Home Music, 1999)

Legends of Rock and Roll (Alpha Video, 1996)

Mondo Elvis (Rhino Home Video, 1990)

This Is Elvis (Warner Bros., 1981)

● DISCOGRAPHY

Elvis: The Complete 50's Masters (RCA 1992)
The Essential 60's Masters I (RCA 1993)
The Sun Record Collection (Rhino Records Inc. 1994)
The Essential 70's Masters (RCA 1995)

● FILMOGRAPHY

Love Me Tender (20th Century Fox 1956)

Loving You (Paramount 1957)

Jailhouse Rock (MGM 1957)

King Creole (Paramount 1958)

G. I. Blues (Paramount 1960)

Flaming Star (20th Century Fox 1960)

Wild in the Country (20th Century Fox 1961)

Blue Hawaii (Paramount 1961)

Follow That Dream (United Artists 1962)

Kid Galahad (United Artists 1962)

Girls! Girls! Girls! (Paramount 1962)

It Happened at the World's Fair (MGM 1963)

Fun in Acapulco (Paramount 1963)

Kissin' Cousins (MGM 1964)

Viva Las Vegas (MGM 1964)

Roustabout (Paramount 1964)

Girl Happy (MGM 1965)

Tickle Me (Allied Artists 1965)

Harum Scarum (MGM 1965)

Frankie and Johnny (United Artists 1966)

Paradise, Hawaiian Style (Paramount 1966)

Spinout (MGM 1966)

Easy Come, Easy Go (Paramount 1967)

Double Trouble (MGM 1967)

Clambake (United Artists 1967)

Stay Away, Joe (MGM 1968)

Speedway (MGM 1968)

Live a Little, Love a Little (MGM 1968)

Charro (National General Pictures 1969)

The Trouble with Girls (and How to Get Into It) (MGM 1969)

Change of Habit (NBC-Universal 1970)

● ACKNOWLEDGMENTS

With a little help from my friends: Mark Teague, Lowry Hamner, Chris Kearin, Kerry McEneny, Kristen Eberle, Liz Szabla, Larry Keeter, Steve Scott, Sarah Longacre, Paula Reedy, Manuela Soares, Kate Lapin, Victoria Maher, and, most especially, Amy Griffin.

● PHOTO CREDITS

Cover: ©Opal Walker, Memphis, TN Pages: ix: Bettmann/Corbis, New York; 4: Courtesy of EPE; 5: Courtesy of EPE; 8: Globe Photos, New York; 10: Courtesy of EPE; 11: Courtesy of EPE; 15: Courtesy of EPE; 16: Courtesy of EPE; 17: Courtesy of EPE; 20: Courtesy of EPE; 24: Courtesy of EPE; 27: G.A. Baker Archives/Redferns/Retna, New York; 28: Mississippi Valley Collection, University of Memphis Libraries, Memphis, TN; 30: Michael Ochs Archive, Venice, CA; 32: Courtesy of EPE; 33: ©Opal Walker, Memphis, TN; 34: Courtesy of EPE; 36: ©1989 Jay: Leviton-Atlanta, GA; 37: Michael Ochs Archive; 38, top: ©1989 Jay: Leviton-Atlanta,; 38, bottom: Courtesy of EPE; 39: Courtesy of EPE; 42: Courtesy of Lansky Bros. and EPE; 46: Hulton/Archive, New York; 53: © Alfred Wertheimer, New York; 54: Photofest, New York; 56: Courtesy of EPE; 58: Globe Photos; 62: Bettmann/Corbis; 66: Michael Ochs Archive; 67: Globe Photos; 72: Bettmann/Corbis: 73: Courtesy of EPE; 78: Courtesy of EPE; 79: Bettmann/Corbis; 83: Bettmann/Corbis; 89: Courtesy of EPE; 90: © Seattle Post-Intelligencer Collection; Museum of History & Industry/Corbis; 91: Bonhams/All Action/Retna; 102: Bettmann/Corbis; 114: Photofest; 115: album cover from the collection of Sarah Longacre; 116: Popperfoto/Archive Photos; 121: courtesy of EPE; 125, top: Bettmann/Corbis; 125, bottom: Archive Photos; 126: UPI/Corbis; 129: Bettmann/Corbis; 132: Joel Axelrad/Retna; 135: courtesy of EPE; 137: courtesy of EPE; 141: AP/Wide World Photos, New York; 145, all: courtesy of EPE; 147: Globe Photos; 148: Harry Siskind/Corbis Outline; 149: People Magazine, New York; 150: courtesy of EPE; 154: ©Ron Galella, Montville, NJ. Elvis Presley and Graceland photos used by permission of Elvis Presley Enterprises, Inc., Memphis, TN. Elvis, Elvis Presley, and Graceland are registered trademarks of EPE. All rights reserved.

Picture Research: Sarah Longacre and Jessica Moon

● SONG CREDITS

"Tupelo Honey" by Van Morrison. Copyright © by Caledonia Soul Music Co./ Warner Bros. Music Corp. ASCAP; "School Days" by Chuck Berry. Copyright © 1957 by Isalee Music Co., BMI; "Memphis" by Chuck Berry. Copyright © 1963 by Isalee Music Co., BMI; "Here Comes the Sun" by George Harrison. Copyright © 1969 by Harrisongs Ltd.; "Sensation" by Pete Townsend. Copyright © Eel Pie Publishing Ltd. (BMI); "Come Together" by John Lennon and Paul McCartney. Copyright © 1969 Northern Songs Ltd; "Money (That's What I Want)" by Berry Gordy Jr. and Janie Bradford. Copyright © 1963 United Partnership Ltd.; "Act Naturally" by Vonie Morrison and Johnny Russell. Copyright © 1965 by EMI Music Publishing Ltd.; "Graceland" by Paul Simon. Copyright ©1986 by Paul Simon. Used by permission of the Publisher: Paul Simon Music; "Ain't Got You" by Bruce Springsteen. Copyright © 1987 by Bruce Springsteen/ASCAP; "San Andreas Fault" by Natalie Merchant. Copyright © 1995 by Indian Love Bride; "Once In a Lifetime" by David Byrne, Brian Eno, Chris Frantz, Jerry Harrison, and Tina Weymouth. Copyright © Index Music, Inc./BLEU Disque Music Co., Inc. ASCAP; "A Man Needs A Maid" by Neil Young. Copyright © 1972 by Broken Arrow Music Publishing/ BMI; "The Times They Are A-Changin'" by Bob Dylan. Copyright © 1963; renewed 1991 Special Rider Music; "Deeper Well" by Dave Olney, Daniel Lanois, Emmylou Harris. Copyright © 1995 by Asylum Records; "Nowhere Man" by John Lennon and Paul McCartney. Copyright © 1965 Northern Songs Ltd.; "Two Faces" by Bruce Springsteen. Copyright © 1987 by Bruce Springsteen/ASCAP; "Not Dark Yet" by Bob Dylan. Copyright © 1996 Special Rider Music; "Trying to Get to Heaven" by Bob Dylan. Copyright © 1996 Special Rider Music.

● INDEX